REPRODUCTIVE JUSTICE, ADOPTION, AND FOSTER CARE

Understanding practices of family separation and child removal necessitates considering the impacts of globalizing capitalism, colonialism, empire building and the establishment and normalization of systemic racism.

In *Reproductive Justice, Adoption, and Foster Care*, the authors situate the colonial legacies of family separation, what it means to center the right parent, and Reproductive Justice and transnational feminist frameworks in conversation with one another in order to elucidate a more nuanced and comprehensive approach to recognizing the significance of contemporary examples of family separation. In doing so, the book showcases the connections between adoption and foster care within the intellectual and activist frameworks of human rights, Critical Adoption Studies, Reproductive Justice, and transnational feminisms. Epistemologically, Reproductive Justice and transnational feminisms meet at the point where both consider and interrogate globalizing capitalism, neoliberal economic and political ideologies, and the ways that various people—mostly people of color, poor people, women, children, and Indigenous people—are considered disposable. Critical Adoption Studies also importantly highlights the ways that adoption and foster care function as forms of family formation and as mechanisms of globalizing capitalism and state formation. Thus, it is critical that any exploration of the reproductive experiences of marginalized individuals interrogate and complicate notions of "choice" to advocate for justice.

Reproductive Justice, Adoption, and Foster Care will be of interest to students of sociology, psychology, and social work, as well as scholars, activists, policymakers, and adoption and foster care practitioners.

Tanya Saroj Bakhru is a professor and program coordinator of the Women, Gender, and Sexuality Studies Program at San Jose State University. She holds a PhD in Women's Studies from University College Dublin in Ireland. Her research focuses on transnational women's health movements and reproductive justice.

Krista L. Benson is an associate professor in the School of Interdisciplinary Studies at Grand Valley State University, teaching in LGBT Studies, Integrative Studies, and Digital Studies. They hold a PhD from The Ohio State University with an interdisciplinary specialization in Sexuality Studies. Their research focuses on how the co-constitution of sexuality, gender, race, and Indigenous sovereignty impacts marginalized people, especially children and young adults, and those involved with the criminal injustice system at all ages.

REPRODUCTIVE JUSTICE, ADOPTION, AND FOSTER CARE

Tanya Saroj Bakhru and Krista L. Benson

Designed cover image: Lizbett Benge

First published 2024
by Routledge
4 Park Square, Milton Park, Abingdon, Oxon OX14 4RN

and by Routledge
605 Third Avenue, New York, NY 10158

Routledge is an imprint of the Taylor & Francis Group, an informa business

© 2024 Tanya Saroj Bakhru and Krista L. Benson

The right of Tanya Saroj Bakhru and Krista L. Benson to be identified as authors of this work has been asserted in accordance with sections 77 and 78 of the Copyright, Designs and Patents Act 1988.

All rights reserved. No part of this book may be reprinted or reproduced or utilised in any form or by any electronic, mechanical, or other means, now known or hereafter invented, including photocopying and recording, or in any information storage or retrieval system, without permission in writing from the publishers.

Trademark notice: Product or corporate names may be trademarks or registered trademarks, and are used only for identification and explanation without intent to infringe.

British Library Cataloguing-in-Publication Data
A catalogue record for this book is available from the British Library

ISBN: 978-1-032-30106-8 (hbk)
ISBN: 978-1-032-30103-7 (pbk)
ISBN: 978-1-003-30344-2 (ebk)

DOI: 10.4324/9781003303442

Typeset in Galliard
by KnowledgeWorks Global Ltd.

CONTENTS

Acknowledgments vii
About the Authors x

1 Introduction 1

    A Transracial Adoptee Writing Herself into
Existence: Interlude with Shannon Gibney 16

2 "Systems of Care" in Foster Care and Adoption 26

    Wrestling with Colonial Legacies of Iñupiaq Family
Separation: Interlude with Roo Ramos 42

3 Transnational Adoption and Indigenous Sovereignty 60

    Constellations of National Economies, Family
Separation, and Military Occupation in the
Transnational Adoption Industrial Complex:
Interlude with Kimberly D. McKee 78

4 Juvenile Justice, Foster Care, and Adoption 91

    Creative Resistance for and by Systems-involved
Young People: Interlude with Lizbett Benge 105

5 Reimagining Care and Community: The Right to Parent   118

Visions of the Future Through Indigenous Human
Rights: Interlude with Julian Aguon   132

Index   *143*

ACKNOWLEDGMENTS

The journey of writing anything, especially a book that crosses so many fields and perspectives, is a labor of community and not individual work. We are immensely grateful to the following people, whose professional expertise was indispensable in completing this project. Thanks to:

- Sara Habein for copyediting and preliminary formatting
- Paige Loughlin, our editor at Routledge, for shepherding this project; Charlotte Taylor at Routledge for her initial interest in the project and coordinating our advance contrac; and the publishing committee at Routledge for their interest in this project
- Lizbett Benge for creating the amazing and striking artwork for the cover of the book.
- Julia Mauriello for assistance in research and copy editing

This project has always been centered around the perspectives of people most impacted by systems of inequality and family removal. Thank you so much to Shannon Gibney, Roo Ramos, Kimberly McKee, Lizbett Benge, and Julian Aguon for the interlude interviews. They provide the backbone of this book, and we cannot imagine it without your contributions.

In addition, thank you to the anonymous peer reviewers who helped shape this proposal and project into the book that you are reading today. This project was also funded in part by Grand Valley State University's Center for Scholarship and Creative Excellence's Collaboration Grant and a GVSU CSCE Mini-Grant.

Krista's Acknowledgements

I would like to start by thanking my family—chosen and biological—for their support across all of my professional and intellectual wanderings. Thank you to my parents, Bob and June Benson, for always supporting my work. Special thanks to Grant Stancliff, my partner, for not only asking me incisive questions but also being willing to read a draft of anything I write and to ask even more questions about that. I wouldn't be who I am today without your support and partnership, G.

I would also like to thank all of the people who supported me in a million ways, including my colleagues whom I met at Grand Valley State University in Integrative Studies (previously Liberal Studies) and now the School of Interdisciplinary Studies and Brooks College of Interdisciplinary Studies more broadly. In particular, I want to thank my comrade such as Jae Basiliere, Dan Cope, Max Counter, Aubrey Dull, Abby Gatreau, Ginele Johnson, Lynnette Keen, Alisha Karabinus, Diana Lamphiere, Daniela Marini, Kimberly McKee, Justin Pettibone, Crystal Scott-Tunstall, Melanie Shell-Weiss, and Ramya Swayamprakash. I also want to thank many of the people who helped shape my perspectives on transnational feminisms, Reproductive Justice, Indigenous sovereignty, and racial justice during my PhD at The Ohio State University, especially Daniel Rivers, Mytheli Sreenivas, and Mary Thomas, whose feedback in courses and conversations fundamentally shaped how I see the world. Thank you, to all of you, for helping shape the larger struggle. I would also like to thank my friends and colleagues Hope Sample, Grant Stancliff, and Aubrey Dull for their early feedback on some of the chapters in this book.

The field research for some of my work is greatly indebted to institutional and archival support. Thank you so much to Linnea Anderson at the Social Welfare History Archives at the University of Minnesota and other archivists who assisted me in my 2016 and 2022 trips to the archives, as well as to Julie Rosicky, CEO of International Social Services, for allowing me access to sealed ISS records. In addition, thank you to the GVSU Fred Meijer Center for Writing & Michigan Authors for the August 2021 Faculty Writing Retreat, where I was able to dedicate time to a sample chapter and revise this book proposal, as well as the Winter 2023 Faculty Writing Retreat, where I was able to work on drafts of Chapters 3 and 4.

Finally, thank you to Tanya Saroj Bahkru for being a comrade, collaborator, and friend. I'm proud to walk this road with you.

Tanya's Acknowledgements

I would like to thank my partner Tina and my son Finn, who have offered me unending support and limitless opportunities to grow and do my human revolution. I would also like to thank Dr. Daisaku Ikeda and the Soka Gakkai International, especially the Alameda West District, for their constant encouragement and guidance to never give up, always choose hope and the reminder that winter never fails to turn to spring. I would also like to thank Krista Benson for being a true collaborator and great friend.

ABOUT THE AUTHORS

Tanya Bakhru
I have been involved in the field of Women, Gender, and Sexuality Studies for over twenty years. From the start, I was drawn to learning and organizing around issues pertaining to the body. The body is a critical site in the struggle for liberation and the ability to determine one's destiny, and its centrality to one's sense of self resonates deeply with me. The body is located at the crossroads of personal and political. Struggles for power, authority, and influence take place over and upon the body, and that translates into the material realities of communities, societies, and nations.

I grew up in a multiracial household marked by the tragedy and trauma of colonization, racism, xenophobia, and fascism. My paternal grandmother was born in India while it was under colonial rule. She married as a young teen and had her first child, who died in infancy. Not too long after, she gave birth to my father. I doubt she had little, if any, say about the intimate, embodied life decisions that shaped her life. When my dad was thirteen years old, he, along with my aunt and my grandmother, was forced to separate from his two brothers and his father as an independent Indian state emerged. These experiences shaped and continue to shape the trajectory of my family's lives into the future. Fast forward two generations, and I find myself the queer parent of an adopted child who came into my life through a story of family separation of his own. Parallels and connections between my son and me, of trauma and resilience, of issues of bodily integrity and self-determination, and the reverberations of the power of the state on and over people's bodies are not lost on me as I look at my own journey into parenthood, the creation and maintenance of family, and the politics that inscribe it. This book is a way for me to work through the complexities that lay within and use my positionality as a researcher, writer, and professor to advocate for justice.

Krista Benson

For more than twenty years, I have been involved as a scholar and activist in fields centered around resisting systems of violence, advocating for Reproductive Justice, and interrogating overlaps between systems of power as they are leveraged against the most vulnerable. Because of these interests, I am often involved and interested in talking to youth and young people about their experiences, centering their knowledge, and recognizing their unique vulnerabilities under United States law. As an activist, I was taught the most effective change occurs when we center the needs and experiences of the most marginalized in our communities.

I am a first-generation college graduate in my family, and I spent my childhood in Montana mostly obsessed with watching people and reading books—a good foundation for a curious child to become an academic. I have found myself invested in work where I am often a guest; I am not an adoptee or a fosteree. I am a white person committed to anti-racist and anti-colonial activism and scholarship. I am a prison abolitionist who has never been incarcerated or jailed. In all of these positions, I am careful to spend a lot of time reading, listening, and learning, especially from those people most directly impacted by systems like adoption, foster care, racism, colonialism, sexism, and racism. While I have never been a foster parent directly, I have served as a parental figure/"bonus adult" to children and young adults who have been raised by my chosen family members. Sometimes these children came into our lives through official foster care channels and sometimes through unofficial family care. For me, this book is a culmination of these experiences and the knowledge created along the way.

1
INTRODUCTION

For too long, activists and scholars engaged in critically examining state systems of "care work," such as adoption and foster care, and those advocating for Reproductive Justice have operated in largely disconnected circles. Though there are exceptions to this, they are too rare.

Reproductive Justice, Adoption, and Foster Care contends that as we critically examine systems of care work through adoption and fostering, the work happening in Critical Adoption Studies, Reproductive Justice, Transnational Feminisms, and human rights must also be a critical part of the conversation. In this primer, we do just that.

Understanding practices of family separation and child removal necessitates considering the impacts of globalizing capitalism, colonialism, and empire building, as well as the establishing and normalizing of systemic racism. This book argues that situating the colonial legacies of family separation, what it means to center the right parent, and Reproductive Justice and Transnational Feminist frameworks in conversation with one another elucidates a more nuanced and comprehensive approach to recognizing the significance and impact of contemporary examples of family separation. This approach makes evident the connections between adoption and foster care with the intellectual and activist frameworks of human rights, Critical Adoption Studies, Reproductive Justice, and Transnational Feminisms. Epistemologically, Reproductive Justice and Transnational Feminisms meet at the point where both consider and interrogate globalizing capitalism, neoliberal economic and political ideologies, and the ways that various people—mostly people of color, poor people, women, children, and Indigenous people—are

DOI: 10.4324/9781003303442-1

considered disposable. These processes work to undermine the public sphere so that social welfare networks "naturalize capitalist values as if they are inevitable."[1] Critical Adoption Studies also importantly connects with Transnational Feminisms and human rights, as the field focuses on how adoption and foster care function not only as forms of family formation but as mechanisms of globalizing capitalism and state formation. Thus, it is critical that any exploration of the reproductive experiences of marginalized individuals interrogate and complicate notions of "choice" to advocate for justice.

In the interests of forwarding this analysis, each of the chapters in this book builds upon one another to both provide a broad framing of adoption and foster care and how they relate to reproductive justice, and also provides examples of case studies. Beginning with framing adoption, foster care, and the Reproductive Justice movement, we then move into applying Transnational Feminist theories and analyses of human rights when considering what systems of state-sponsored and -managed "care" look like. After that, we focus on two case studies of little-understood parts of foster care and adoption in the United States—the connections between the transnational adoption project of Korean "orphans" into the United States after the Korean War and the establishment of the Indian Adoption Project, when Indigenous children were placed in white homes far from their communities. We then interrogate the overlap between foster care, adoption from foster care, and the juvenile justice system that occurs in the legal category of "in-state care." Finally, we reconsider the notion of ethics of care and communities that center the right to parent as a human right. This chapter highlights some organizations and movements seeking to abolish the foster care system as we know it today. *Reproductive Justice, Adoption, and Foster Care* is dedicated to centering the voices of those most impacted by these systems, and we employ careful citational practices that privilege the knowledge of first parents, adoptees, people of color, and Indigenous people. Additionally, we also prioritize the experiences and knowledge of people directly impacted by child removal, systemic racism, and colonization through our interlude interviews with adoptees, survivors of the foster care system, first parents, and decolonial Indigenous activists. From the original conception of this book, the interviews included in this volume were central to this project for both of us, as the voices of these people directly impacted by the systems that we historicize and theorize in this volume are vital to understanding these issues. Hearing the expertise of human rights attorneys, creative writers, adoptees, and former fosterees, as well as their own personal experiences, deepen our fuller understanding of these systems, their impacts, and how people creatively survive and even thrive despite them.

Brief History of Foster Care and Adoption

The establishment of a family court system in the United States emerged during the Progressive Era around the turn of the twentieth century. Prior to this time, there was not a single system that cohesively addressed questions of child custody, formal adoption, neglect or abuse of children, or acts of juvenile misconduct. During the early 1900s, advocates for child welfare envisioned a comprehensive movement aimed at improving the well-being of children. This movement involved establishing juvenile courts, fighting against child labor, enforcing compulsory school attendance for all students, and establishing both charitable and government agencies dedicated to ensuring the safety and welfare of children.[2] This movement resulted in the establishment of what would become family courts, which would manage child custody, the foster care system, and the juvenile justice system. The intertwining of these systems continues past their implementation, and they highlight how different adoption and foster care are from other forms of family formation.

The systems that we've described here are ones that many refer to as "child welfare" systems. However, following scholars such as Dorothy Roberts and Laura Briggs, we instead prefer to refer to the court systems themselves or to call these systems "child-taking systems," especially when referring to foster care and adoptions that result from foster care in the United States. This term centers the extensive classist, racist, and colonial violence of these systems.[3] The outcomes of the children who are put into these child-taking systems demonstrate this violence. Despite decades of activism to address the disproportionate presence of children of color in foster care—especially Black, Indigenous, and Latine children—recent demographic studies show that those children are still disproportionately taken into the foster care system and that this likelihood compounds over their childhoods. According to a 2015 study, approximately 15% of Indigenous children would enter foster care over their childhoods before the age of 18. Around 11% of Black youth would enter foster care. Less than 5% of white youth would be in state care as minors.[4]

Transnational adoption, much like domestic foster care, has startling patterns around race, ethnicity, and adoption. Scholars have spent a great deal of time drawing connections between militarism, war, economic impacts, and the increased availability of children open for adoption in Latin America, Africa, and Asia.[5] These insights broadly show us that many of the situations that disrupt economic patterns limit access to kinship networks, and war often directly leads to more children from those countries becoming offered up for adoption, and nearly all that are adopted by U.S. parents are adopted by white families. Thus, Black and brown children become potential commodities for the fulfillment of white Americans' desires for a nuclear family, sometimes directly as a result of the U.S.' imperialism.

These systems, while appearing to be neutral legal processes, have been established through, and continue to justify, racism, colonialism, sexism, homophobia, classism, and ableism. It is not an accident that so many of the children who are adopted, fostered, or involved in the juvenile justice system who were born in the United States are from Black, Indigenous, or Latine communities; poor families; young parents; and/or families impacted by disability or addiction. These systems were designed to, on one hand, offer a kind of "benign" paternalism through the child-taking system in a way that is so often violent, or they presented the alternative of detaining children in juvenile courts.

Through the cover of neutrality of adoption and foster care processes in legal structure, the larger public, who has never interacted with these systems, is allowed to see them as the exact "child saving" that the child-savers of the late nineteenth century and many current professionals in these systems wanted people to see. It also obscures the deeply troubling roots of these systems and their impacts. It isn't that all adoptions and foster situations are violent, but rather that these legal processes are based on worldviews that believe that taking children from their families of origin is a better idea than supporting those families, especially when they are particular *kinds* of families. This produces a hierarchy of acceptable families in our collective imagination, which has the outcome of continuing to understand these systems as always for the benefit of the children. We contend that the reality is much more complex.

Reproductive Justice and Transnational Feminisms

Reproductive Justice is an intersectional, human rights-based framework that "makes the link between the individual and community, addresses government and corporate responsibility, fights all forms of population control (eugenics), commits to individual/community leadership development that results in power shifts, and puts marginalized communities at the center of the analysis."[6] While the Reproductive Justice movement is rooted in the work and lived experiences of African American women, it involves theory, strategy, and practice that can apply to everyone. As such, the movement brings American reproductive politics into rhythm with work already being done by feminist groups around the world.

Reproductive Justice offers a holistic model of theory and activism focused on three principles: (1) the right not to have children; (2) the right to have children; and (3) the right to parent children one already has. It points to the sense that "our collective sexual consciousness has been warped by misogyny, slavery, and colonialism."[7] Reproductive Justice centers on the experiences of Black women in America. It also brings to light the ways that systems of oppression like white supremacy, sexism, and capitalism work together in determining the worth, utility, and value of certain bodies over others—a framework that is wide-reaching and illuminating when we understand it in a transnational context.

The epistemological trajectory of Reproductive Justice intersects with Transnational Feminisms, as both paradigms place an interrogation of current-day globalization and neoliberal economic ideology at the center of analysis. Globalization and neoliberal economic ideology aim to undermine the public sphere and position capitalist values as if they are natural and inevitable.[8] As a result, we can no longer afford to speak about reproductive health in terms of *choice*, as is common to do, since the choice referred to is both illusory and secondary to the aims of the state. In order to effectively advocate for justice, it is critical that any exploration of the reproductive experiences of gender and sexual minorities interrogate and complicate notions of "*choice*."

The processes and circumstances that inform how individuals and communities perceive and negotiate their sexual and reproductive freedoms are obscured by the self-propulsion of a global state. As academic and activist Andrea Smith so succinctly articulates, when we rely on *choice* as our main framework for understanding reproductive and sexual experiences, reproductive health matters become configured from a commodity perspective.[9] Through this commodification, the real processes and circumstances that inform how individuals and communities perceive and negotiate their sexual and reproductive freedoms are obscured. When reproductive rights are embedded in notions of *free choice*, all the social, political, and economic factors that surround how choices are made and just how free those choices, in fact, feel become hidden behind the well-accepted principle of individual liberty. In addition, when approaching reproductive health from a commodity perspective, the notion that people have inherent rights is lost. What remains is the idea that choices should only be made if one can afford them or if one is deemed a legitimate choice-maker.[10] Examples of this ideology play out time and again in varying historical and geographic contexts. Against a global backdrop of colonialism, exploitation, and economic, social, and political disenfranchisement that carry on through generations, we need more than choices. We need justice.

Reproductive Justice brings to light the ways that systems of oppression like white supremacy, sexism, and capitalism work together in determining the worth, utility, and value of certain bodies over others, as well as the ways in which children become a kind of currency in this system. The resultant need for justice very much coincides with the aims of

Transnational Feminist frameworks. Transnational Feminist frameworks are committed to addressing the asymmetries of globalization/capitalist re-colonization, as well as the implementation of an intersectional set of understandings, tools, and practices like paying attention to the raced, classed, and gendered ways that globalization and capitalist patriarchies restructure colonial and neo-colonial relations of domination and subordination. As Bakhru discusses in her previous work on the subject, Transnational Feminist scholarship acknowledges the simultaneously constituting relationships between the local and global, employs tools of constant contextualization and historicization, and challenges hegemonic views of global capitalism.[11] Transnational Feminisms also grapples with the complex and contradictory ways that individual and collective agencies are shaped by, and in turn shape, processes of globalization. The framework juxtaposes gender and sexual minorities in similar contexts, in different geographical spaces, rather than as a homogenous category across the world.[12] In a Transnational Feminist framework, contexts, links, and relationships that are material and temporal between the local and global take our focus. As Chandra Mohanty states, "[w]hat is emphasized are relations of mutuality, co-responsibility, and common interests, anchoring the idea of feminist solidarity."[13] It is through such conceptual reconfigurations of pressing issues that we can create and sustain movements for justice and social transformation.

Over the past several decades, a visible transnational women's health movement has emerged and gathered momentum. Responding to the negative impacts of globalization, the rise of antifeminist and fundamentalist political and religious forces, and the HIV/AIDS pandemic, transnational coalitions formed and leadership emerged from the Global South.[14] United Nations conferences, such as the International Conference on Population and Development (ICPD) in 1994 and The World Conference on Women in 1995, along with the non-governmental organizations associated with those conferences, recognized sexual and reproductive health as crucial and complex concepts, among them the control and decision-making over one's body, and the full realization of gender equality.[15] These conferences strengthened the connections between gender equality, justice, education for women, and girls' empowerment and reproductive health. The ICPD, in particular, "emphasized the ineluctable relationship between poverty, underdevelopment, and women's reproduction."[16] In fact, many of the founders of the Reproductive Justice movement in the United States participated in the 1994 ICPD, and they found solidarity with women from the Global South who were already implementing a human rights framework to push back against the forces of globalization and the use of women's fertility as a means to neoliberal economic ends.[17]

In finding feminist solidarity, transnational women's health movements have, in recent years, moved to investigate the interconnections between different communities of women and gender minorities and now look for the "broader pattern and structures of domination and exploitation."[18] If scholars, activists, or policymakers fail to see the points of connection between various groups of people, we run the risk of interpreting sexual and reproductive experiences as only occurring at the individual level, or as entirely private matters. By using Reproductive Justice and Transnational Feminisms as theoretical lenses, our aim is to show a history of lived experiences, both reproductive and sexual, that connect people across time and place within the context of forced family separation disguised as systems of care.

Furthermore, Reproductive Justice and Transnational Feminisms are theoretical and conceptual foundations that are necessary for us to deconstruct the ways in which we think about many different kinds of family separation, including foster care and adoption.

Family separation is both a Transnational Feminist issue and Reproductive Justice issue. The issue speaks to the heart of one's right to have children and to raise those children, and draws our attention to the historical, political, and economic contexts that create and sustain family separation in its various forms. Using Reproductive Justice and Transnational Feminisms to examine family separation practices means that we must acknowledge the ways racism, and white supremacy in particular, along with capitalism and patriarchy work together across time and space. It means that we must historicize and contextualize our understanding of this issue and acknowledge that the United States has a long history of using family separation to ensure state and corporate (or as is becoming ever more prevalent, corporate state) economic, political, and social interests. This book was framed by a fundamental question: how can Reproductive Justice and Transnational Feminisms lenses be used together, as analytical tools, to help us make sense of adoption and foster care in a globalized era?

Dobbs v. Jackson Women's Health Organization and the Indian Child Welfare Act

At the time of writing this book, the United States has entered a new, deeply dystopian phase of its war on women and its attempts to regulate and control bodies on the margins. In June 2022, the Supreme Court ruled to end federal-level protection for abortion in its decision in *Dobbs v. Jackson Women's Health Organization*,[19] overturning the 1973 landmark case *Roe v. Wade*.[20] The *Dobbs* ruling additionally overturned *Planned Parenthood v. Casey*,[21] a case that reinforced the constitutional right to abortion.

The full consequences of the Dobbs decision will no doubt unfold over the course of coming generations and will impact other rights couched in the constitutional right to privacy guaranteed by *Roe,* such as the right to marry a person of the same sex or the right to contraception. The *Dobbs* ruling punted the regulation of abortion down to the state level, immediately causing chaos, extreme disparity in abortion access between states, and a ripple effect that has increased hardship, risk, and even death for all pregnant persons regardless of whether they sought to terminate their pregnancy or not.

A key part of the majority's opinion rested on the idea that adoption can and will remedy the consequences of lack of access to abortion. In the majority opinion, Justice Alito writes, "[S]tates have increasingly adopted 'safe haven' laws, which generally allow women to drop off babies anonymously; and that a woman who puts her newborn up for adoption today has little reason to fear that the baby will not find a suitable home."[22] This argument assumes that adoption is an overwhelmingly positive act. It ignores the ways in which family separation and child removal are traumatic for a multitude of people involved and how it negatively impacts the individual, the family, and the community. One wonders what Justice Alito imagines when he invokes the idea of a "suitable home"? Also, if there are so many "suitable homes" in existence, why are so many children, and children of color in particular, in foster care? The logic is coded in language that invokes a heteronormative white supremacist patriarchal point of view.

As the dissent in *Dobbs* points out, "[M]oreover, the choice to give up parental rights after giving birth is altogether different from the choice not to carry a pregnancy to term."[23] Few of those who are denied an abortion will turn to adoption as an alternative and many will be burdened with a disproportionate share of child care and parenting. That the majority opinion of the court sees adoption as a solution to the lack of availability of abortion is troubling, harmful, and deluded. Assuming that adoption will fix the problem of unintended pregnancy completely ignores the multitude of reasons people seek abortion services, and it ignores the ways that adoption has been a weaponized tool to maintain white supremacist capitalist patriarchy in both a local and global context. It ignores the harms and traumas of adoption, undermines the human rights of women and pregnant people, and severs one's ability to have bodily autonomy and be self-determined. All of these points will be addressed in more detail in the body of this book.

At a fundamentally disturbing level, the Court's originalist reading of the constitution erases women and pregnant people completely from the body politic. As Malinda Seymore states, "Originalism insists that the current Constitution provides no more protection for rights than it did at its framing, a time when women had no vote, no right to own property, no right to custody of their own children, no right to earned wages, and, according to the Court, no right to bodily autonomy or reproductive decision-making."[24] Her thoughts echo the dissenting justices in the *Dobbs* case. "[The Court] says that from the very moment of fertilization, a woman has no rights to speak of. A State can force her to bring a pregnancy to term, even at the steepest personal and familial costs."[25] Justices Breyer, Sotomayor, and Kagan go on to state,

> [W]hatever the exact scope of the coming laws, one result of today's decision is certain: the curtailment of women's rights, and of their status as free and equal citizens.
>
> Yesterday, the Constitution guaranteed that a woman confronted with an unplanned pregnancy could (within reasonable limits) make her own decision about whether to bear a child, with all the life-transforming consequences that act involves. And in thus safeguarding each woman's reproductive freedom, the Constitution also protected '[t]he ability of women to participate equally in [this Nation's] economic and social life.' ... But no longer. As of today, this Court holds, a State can always force a woman to give birth, prohibiting even the earliest abortions. A State can thus transform what, when freely undertaken, is a wonder into what, when forced, may be a nightmare.[26]

And indeed, for many in the post-*Roe* world, their reproductive experiences have been living nightmares—psychological trauma, severe physical illness, and even death.[27] The implications of the *Dobbs* decision warrant an examination beyond the scope of this book, many books' worth indeed.[28] No doubt, we will see discussion continuing to emerge in the near future.

All of the news about recognition of reproductive justice is not bad, however. On June 15, 2023, the U.S. Supreme Court handed down a decision in *Haaland v. Brakeen* that supported the constitutionality and application of ICWA. This case, initiated by Texas, Louisiana, and Indiana, along with individual plaintiffs, called into question ICWA's constitutionality regarding the placement preferences of Indigenous children with Indigenous families. In a decision that surprised us and many Indian Country law experts, one of the most politically conservative and reactionary Supreme Courts in recent U.S. history upheld ICWA, and the majority opinion supported the recognition of Indigenous sovereignty and upheld that supporting that sovereignty necessarily involved the right of Indigenous families and communities to raise their own children.

It cannot be stated strongly enough that now, more than ever, we need a framework to understand and advocate for reproductive freedom that is holistic, intersectional, and rooted in human rights. We need this centered on understandings of human rights and Transnational Feminisms. We need Reproductive Justice.

Overview of the Chapters

Chapter 2: "Systems of Care" in Foster Care and Adoption

Chapter 2 traces the legacies of white settler colonialism, family separation, and the creation of a corporate state. The chapter addresses connections between colonial projects of the past, contemporary globalization, and the role of family separation by highlighting historical examples of the separation of Black families under enslavement, the implementation of Indian boarding schools, and contemporary United States. family separation. The chapter demonstrates to the reader that, in order to fully understand foster care and adoption systems in the present, we must look to the past and realize that controlling the reproductive potential of Black, Indigenous, and people of color is central to the formation of the United States itself.

The chapter begins with a discussion of Reproductive Justice and Transnational Feminist frameworks as analytical tools and shows how they can be used to better understand family separation and respond to the need for justice, Reproductive Justice in particular. Reproductive Justice offers a holistic model of theory and activism focused on three principles: (1) the right not to have children; (2) the right to have children; and (3) the right to parent children one already has. It points to the sense that "our collective sexual consciousness has been warped by misogyny, slavery, and colonialism."[29] While Reproductive Justice centers the experiences of Black women in the United States, it also brings to light the ways that systems of oppression like white supremacy, sexism, and capitalism work together in determining the worth, utility, and value of certain bodies over others, as well as the ways in which children become a kind of currency in this system.[30] This quest for justice very much coincides with Transnational Feminist frameworks. Transnational Feminist frameworks include a commitment to addressing the asymmetries of globalization/capitalist re-colonization, as well as the implementation of an intersectional set of understandings, tools, and practices, such as paying attention to the raced, classed, and gendered ways that globalization and capitalist patriarchies restructure colonial and neo-colonial relations of domination and subordination. As Mohanty states, "What is emphasized are relations of mutuality, co-responsibility, and common interests, anchoring the idea of feminist solidarity."[31]

The last half of the chapter will briefly detail family separation of enslaved Africans, Indian boarding schools, and the family separation policies of the Trump administration. The chapter will show how, in each of these instances, white supremacist capitalist ideologies drove and maintained the interests of the United States by way of configuring children as commodities to be extracted. By demonstrating the use of Reproductive Justice and Transnational Feminist frameworks to understand these examples, the reader will be prepared to think critically about foster care and adoption as it is presented in subsequent chapters.

Chapter 3: Transnational Adoption and Indigenous Sovereignty

Chapter 3 considers the centrality of race and sovereignty in both understanding adoption and foster care, and the relationship that transnational adoption and adoption of Indigenous children has in the establishment and justification of the state in a U.S. context. Building on Chapter2, this chapter considers how the project of empire in the United States and connected wars and military projects have impacted adoption practices, including the examples of the Korean War and the presence of Korean adoptees in the United States, connections between the Korean Adoption Project and the Indian Adoption Project, and how these projects have impacted.

U.S. and Korean domestic policies and adoption policies. These two adoption projects are one of many examples demonstrating the far-reaching effects of U.S. imperialism. Additionally, the connections of these projects highlight something often not recognized within the United States—that because of Indigenous sovereignty, any adoption of an Indigenous child outside of their nation is, much like the adoption of Korean children into other nations, a transnational adoption.

The chapter begins by exploring two seemingly disconnected U.S. governmental projects—the Indian Adoption Project (1955–1978) and the Korean Adoption Project (1950–present day). Both programs were supported by the U.S. government in the aftermath of closing Indian boarding schools, for the former, and the Korean War, for the latter. While the Korean adoption program persists for more than sixty years, this chapter focuses on the program's height in the 1970s and 1980s. This analysis examines the ways that family disruption and state rehoming of children served as justifications for U.S. imperialism projects, wherein children adopted into U.S. homes—nearly entirely into white U.S. families—served as national signals for "peace" and "progress." This chapter situates archival documents concerning both adoption projects into the broader context of changing federal, state, and tribal laws and statutes, attending to the impacts these policy changes had on child welfare for both Indigenous and Korean children and on their families of origin. Indigenous feminist and Transnational Feminist perspectives inform this analysis as this chapter interrogates child removal and the denial of some Indigenous and Korean families' ability to parent in favor of having those children parented by white Americans as a key part of U.S. nation-building.

Chapter 4: Juvenile Justice, Foster Care, and Adoption

This chapter critically examines the category of "in state care" and its overlap with the ways that the juvenile justice system, foster care, and domestic adoption operate and are legally structured in the United States. As explained by scholars, this category is broader than many non-specialists understand. This is because:

> The foster care population is a limited sample of the children for whom the state is responsible. Children who have been placed in state custody or under state supervision are also placed in family homes (their homes of origin, relatives, or other kinship care), sometimes with a formal foster care designation, if in kinship care, but often not.
>
> Children and youth in state custody also are placed in group homes, mental hospitals, and juvenile correctional facilities. By focusing only on children in foster care, a limited and perhaps skewed view is developed.[32]

Additionally, the juvenile non-offender category covers youth in foster care, youth with dependency petitions, and it is overseen by juvenile court judges.

This chapter traces the historical and contemporary overrepresentation of Indigenous youth and youth of color in U.S. foster care, group homes, mental hospitals, and under the supervision of the juvenile justice systems. We examine the establishment of both juvenile courts and the foster care systems and how those resulting connected systems during the Progressive Era—at the impetus of wealthy, white "child savers" who were concerned about the status of poor youth, youth of color, and Indigenous youth — sentenced those youth through the adult criminal justice system.[33] Like many other projects of the Progressive Era (e.g. the Orphan Train movement), this project was driven by the goal of assimilating and controlling poor white families, families of color, and Indigenous families with the veneer of saviorism. These projects can only be understood if we understand them as woven into the U.S. projects of imperialism through a Transnational Feminist and Reproductive Justice analysis.

The second half of the chapter examines the webs of interconnected systems that continue to try to "save" poor white children, Indigenous children, and children of color by separating them from their families of origin—including the juvenile justice system, foster care, and adoption from foster care—into predominantly middle class, white homes. Juvenile justice and foster care are both systems that are managed and regulated at the state and county level, meaning that there are anywhere between fifty and more than one thousand different iterations of these systems, their rules, and guidelines for how youth should or can be treated. This complex web of systems means that the youth who are most likely to be under state family surveillance, and thus put into these systems, are also more likely to be separated from their families through these systems. This chapter demonstrates that when Reproductive Justice theory and practice are applied to these systems, the most compelling option is abolition of our current juvenile justice and foster care systems, to be supplanted with supportive programs for families, reallocation of resources to impoverished communities, and community-run and community-accountable processes to ensure the well-being of children in our communities.

Chapter 5: Reimagining Care and Community: The Right to Parent

A central tenet of the Reproductive Justice framework is the right to parent the children one already has in a safe and healthy environment. This principle is based on the idea that parenting is a human right as outlined in the Universal Declaration of Human Rights. This chapter begins by exploring the idea of the right to parent as rooted in human rights discourse and demonstrates the ways in which the right to parent is directly related to the health and safety of one's community. The notion of the right to parent in a safe and healthy environment demands that "the state not unduly interfere with women's reproductive decision making, but it also insists that the state has an obligation to help create the conditions for women to exercise their decisions without coercion and with social supports."[34] This chapter traces the formation of the right to parent as a human right and addresses what it might take to realize an individual's right to parent.

The second half of this chapter provides three short case studies of organizations working to stop family separation and reimagine notions of family, community, and care. Case studies include *upEND*, an organization working on abolition of the foster care system; *Families Belong Together*, an organization that works to permanently end family separation and detention and seeks accountability for the harm that has been done; and *Movement for Family Power,* an organization focused on divestment from the foster system and reinvestment in community.

Through the examination of these organizations, this chapter ties together key ideas from the book as a whole: the colonial legacy of family separation, the importance of Reproductive Justice and Transnational Feminist frameworks to comprehensively understand the significance and impact of family separation, and what it means to center the right to parent as we move forward in building a new future where all children and families are truly valued.

Notes

1. Loretta Ross, Lynn Roberts, Erika Derkas, Whitney Peoples, and Pamela Bridgewater Toure, eds., *Radical Reproductive Justice: Foundations, Theory, Practice, Critique* (New York: Feminist Press at the City University of New York, 2017), 199.
2. Dorothy E. Roberts, *Shattered Bonds: The Color of Child Welfare* (New York: Basic, 2002) and Walter I. Trattner, *From Poor Law to Welfare State: A History of Social Welfare in America* (Chicago: University of Chicago Press), 1989.
3. Dorothy E. Roberts, "Keynote: How I became a family policing abolitionist." *Columbia Journal of Race and Law* 11, no. 3 (2021): 455–469; Laura Briggs, "Twentieth century Black and Native activism against the child taking system: Lessons for the present." *Columbia Journal of Race and Law* 11, no. 3 (2021): 611–638.
4. Christopher Wildeman and Natalia Emanuel, "Cumulative risks of foster care placement by age 18 for U.S. children, 2000–2011." *PLoS ONE* 9, no. 3 (2014): e92785.
5. For a small sample, see: Laura Briggs, *Somebody's Children: The Politics of Transracial and Transnational Adoption* (Durham: Duke University Press, 2012); Kimberly McKee, *Disrupting Kinship: Transnational Politics of Korean Adoption in the United States* (Champaign: University of Illinois Press, 2019).
6. Loretta Ross, Lynn Roberts, Erika Derkas, Whitney Peoples, and Pamela Bridgewater Toure, eds., *Radical Reproductive Justice: Foundations, Theory, Practice, Critique* (New York: Feminist Press at the City University of New York, 2017), 19.
7. Ross, et al., *Radical Reproductive Justice*, 175.
8. Ross, et al., *Radical Reproductive Justice*, 21.
9. Andrea Smith, "Beyond pro-choice versus pro-life: Women of color and reproductive justice," *NWSA Journal* 17, no. 1 (Spring 2005): 119–140. https://www.jstor.org/stable/i400036.
10. Smith, "Beyond pro-choice versus pro-life."
11. Tanya S. Bakhru, "Negotiating and navigating the rough terrain of transnational feminist research," *Journal of International Women's Studies* 10, no. 2 (January 2008): https://scholarworks.sjsu.edu/cgi/viewcontent.cgi?article=1000&context=soc_sci_pub, 198–216; Kum-Kum Bhavani and Molly Talcott, "Interconnections and configurations: Toward a global feminist perspective," in *Handbook of Feminist Research*, ed. Sharlene Nagy Hesse-Biber (Thousand Oaks: SAGE Publications, 2007), 135–153; Hyung Sook Kim, "The Politics of Border Crossings: Black, Postcolonial, and Transnational Feminist Perspectives," in Nagy Hesse-Biber, *Handbook of Feminist Research*; and Maria Mies, "A Global Feminist Perspective on Research," in Nagy Hesse-Biber, *Handbook of Feminist Research*.
12. Richa Nagar and Amanda L. Swarr, "Theorizing Transnational Feminist Praxis," in *Critical Transnational Feminist Praxis*, Swarr and Nagar, eds. (New York: State University of New York Press, 2010), 1–20.
13. Chandra Talpade Mohanty, *Feminism Without Borders: Decolonizing Theory, Practicing Solidarity* (Durham: Duke University Press, 2003), 242.

14 Rosalind P. Petchesky, *Global Prescriptions: Gendering Health and Human Rights* (New York: Zed Books, 2003), 1.
15 United Nations, *Programme of Action Adopted at the ICPD: Cairo, 5–13 September 1994* (New York: United Nations Population Fund, 1994), https://www.unfpa.org/publications/interna tional-conference-population-and-development-programme-action.
16 Ross, et al., *Radical Reproductive Justice*, 43.
17 Ross, et al., *Radical Reproductive Justice*, 44.
18 Mohanty, *Feminism Without Borders*, 967.
19 *Dobbs v. Jackson Women's Health Organization*, No. 19-1392, 597 U.S. (2022), chrome- extension://efaidnbmnnnibpcajpcglclefindmkaj/https://www.supremecourt.gov/opinions/21pdf/19-1392_6j37.pdf.
20 *Roe v. Wade*, 410 U.S. 113 (1973).
21 *Planned Parenthood v. Casey*, 505 U.S. 833 (1992).
22 *Dobbs*, 34.
23 *Dobbs*, 40.
24 Seymore, Malinda l. "Originalism: Erasing women from the body politic." *Adoption & Culture* 10, no. 2 (2022): 214–219, doi:10.1353/ado.2022.0019.
25 *Dobbs* (Breyer, Sotomayor and Kagan dissenting), 2.
26 *Dobbs* (Breyer, Sotomayor and Kagan dissenting), 4.
27 *Dobbs* (Breyer, Sotomayor and Kagan dissenting), 4, citing *Casey*, 856.
28 Frances Sellers, Thomas Simonetti and Maggie Penman, "The Short Life of Baby Milo," *The Washington Post*, May 19, 2023, https://www.washingtonpost.com/health/interactive/2023/florida-abortion-law-deborah-dorbert/?itid=lk_interstitial_manual_8; Sarah McCammon, "5 Texas Women Denied Abortions Sue the State, Saying the Bans Put Them in Danger," NPR.org, updated March 8, 2023, https://www.npr.org/2023/03/07/1161486096/abortion-texas-lawsuit-Women-sue-dobbs; Oriana Gonzáles, "Dobbs decision is 'devastating' U.S. maternal health, Biden ddministration Says," Axios.com, Health, December 14, 2002, https://www.axios.com/2022/12/14/maternal-deaths-dobbs-abortions-us-health.
29 Ross, et al., *Radical Reproductive Justice*, 19.
30 Ross, et al., *Radical Reproductive Justice*, 175.
31 Mohanty, *Feminism Without Borders*, 242.
32 Craig Anne Heflinger, Celeste G. Simpkins, and Terri Combs-Orme. "Using the CBCL to determine the clinical status of children in state custody." *Children and youth services review* 22, no. 1 (2000): 55–73, 63.
33 Thomas J. Bernard and Megan C. Kurlychek, *Global Prescriptions: Gendering Health and Human Rights* (New York: Oxford University Press, 2010), 48–94.
34 Ross, et al., *Radical Reproductive Justice*, p. 169.

A TRANSRACIAL ADOPTEE WRITING HERSELF INTO EXISTENCE

Interlude with Shannon Gibney

Shannon Gibney is a writer, educator, activist, and the author of *See No Color* (Carolrhoda Lab, 2015) and *Dream Country* (Dutton, 2018) young adult novels that won the Minnesota Book Awards in 2016 and 2019. Gibney is faculty in English at Minneapolis College, where she teaches writing; she was recently selected as one of three Educators of the Year in the entire Minnesota State College and University system. A Bush Artist and McKnight Writing Fellow, her new novel, *The Girl I Am, Was, and Never Will Be*, explores themes of transracial adoption through speculative memoirs (Dutton, 2023). Gibney's other recent publications include the picture books *Sam and the Incredible African* and *American Food Fight* (University of Minnesota Press, 2023) and *Where We Come From* (Lerner, 2022; coauthored), and *When We Become Ours: A YA Adoptee Anthology* (HarperTeen, 2023), co-edited with Nicole Chung.

Tanya Bakhru: Thank you for sitting down with us. This first question is just kind of to give the readers an introduction to you and some context. What brought you to the work that you do now?

Shannon Gibney: I identify as a mixed Black transracial adoptee. I was adopted by a white couple in Ann Arbor, Michigan, in 1975. Of course, as human beings, we have many different intersectional identities, but for me, I feel like my identity as a transracially adopted woman in a certain time period is the biggest marker of my identity and experience. In terms of the way that I move through the world, the way that I see myself, the way that I see others, the way that I see identity, my ideas about community, and certainly my imagination, all those things have been, I would say, indeed will be shaped by my experience as a mixed Black transracially adopted woman. I'm also a writer, I'm also a scholar and teacher. I teach at Minneapolis College, which is a two-year community college in downtown Minneapolis. I've taught there for about twelve or thirteen years now. In my writing, I have penned some critical adoption studies scholarship, but most of what I do certainly is creative writing. My first book, See *No Color*,[1] is very much based on my personal experience as a mixed Black transracial adoptee. It's about a mixed Black girl adopted into a white family, and it's a coming-of-age story, and it's all about race, power, identity, belonging, gender, all of these things. My new book, *The Girl I Am, Was, and Never Will Be: A Speculative Memoir of Transracial Adoption*,[2] really is probably the most autobiographical thing I've written, although it is also probably the weirdest thing I've ever written as well, because I've got all kinds of pictures from my birth families, I've got pictures from my adopted families, I've got my birth father's birth certificate, I've got all kinds of things in there. When I was in my late twenties, I moved to Minneapolis. The Twin Cities is known as the land of 10,000 Korean adoptees. The state motto is the land of 10,000 lakes. So that's like a funny take on that. I think I didn't know; I knew that I was adopted, but I didn't know that I was an adoptee until I met them. That was a really pivotal moment in my own personal education around the history and politics of transracial adoption. I don't mean to flatten the experience and say that my experience as a domestic Black adoptee is exactly like an internationally adopted Korean adoptee because it's not. But, certainly, the experiences of isolation, dislocation, racism, and questions about racial shame, too, are very similar.

Krista Benson: I have a follow-up question on that. I'm really interested. You said the sentence, "I knew I was adopted, but I didn't know I was an adoptee." Could you tell me a little bit about the distinction that you see between those or what that sentence says to you?

Gibney: Right, so there were always people, other kids who were transracial adoptees, like in my school, there weren't like a ton of them, but I kind of knew them for sure. Like, "Oh, Daniel, yes, he's adopted from Columbia, his mom's white." Or "Oh, there's like, these two siblings, I remember, and they were both adopted from India, I believe." But there was never a moment of acknowledgement, right? Like, I always think of Black people, if you're in any kind of if you're in most social settings, particularly like white social settings, and you see another Black person, there's just this silent recognition, and sometimes not silent, like, hey, like the head nod, right? That was not a thing, not surprisingly, because of the structural isolation of us adopted children that we wouldn't do the recognition, like "Oh, you're adopted too, you're a transracial adoptee. Yeah. Your parents are white, and you're brown too, and you were adopted, and like, what does that mean?" That never happened. Being an adoptee as a category of identity, as a category of significant meaning did not come into my consciousness again until I met all these other adoptees, many of whom politicized and educated me about the history of transracial adoption in general, and then from there, Korean adoption in particular.

Benson: Awesome. Thank you. This articulation, I don't think it's come up in our interviews so far, and I think it's a really important one, so I appreciate you clarifying that. Our next question is, how have you seen the ways that adoption and foster care are talked about change over the time that you've worked on these issues?

Gibney: Yeah, that is a great question. I think definitely in the past three to five years, I have seen a significant shift, certainly in the way people talk about foster care or just people talking about foster care at all. I just feel like there's just this silent box of foster care that nobody really goes into when we talk about child welfare issues. There's also just been some really incredible journalism that's come out and investigative reports all about how the system is corrupt, like, just not functioning and is violent towards kids, all of these things.[3] I do feel like there's much more awareness around the fact that foster care is not good. It's not a good system. It doesn't do what it says that it's supposed to do in terms of family preservation. It creates more trauma for kids, not less, most of the time. Right. Like Dorothy Roberts' book, *Shattered Bonds*.[4] She's an amazing scholar. To have somebody come out with a full-fledged book on the topic of foster care and detailing how child welfare is another arm of the state. Other people have said that, but just use that framework, I guess, particularly in this moment with people really struggling with the ongoing police violence against Black people and what are alternatives to that, right? So, what are alternatives to foster care? That's a real important question that I don't see very many people grappling with.

I've met so many incredible people, many of them scholars, many of them adoptees – I should say adoptee scholars. I mean, there wasn't a field called Critical Adoption Studies years ago. It just didn't exist. My favorite conference is ASAC, the Alliance for the Study of Adoption and Culture. It's a biennial conference, and it's small. It's usually like 120, maybe 200 people, but they bring folks who study adoption in popular discourse from all over the world. That is where I met Kim McKee. I've met so many incredible people, many of them scholars, many of them adoptees. The amount of connections that I've just been able to leverage and make has been phenomenal, and obviously, it's longitudinal through the years. I do think that probably about 15 years ago, there started to be a real critical mass of us transracial adoptees who were coming of age and trying to talk about adoption in these more complex ways instead of just like, well, are you for it or are you against it, which really annoys adoptees. But that's what the framework usually is. When I was like a teenager or in my early 20s, there was almost no literature on adoption or foster care. I think that there's a framework now and digital communities as well that have opened things up so that some of the structural barriers to finding other adoptees have been lifted. And building specific communities, let's say, within your racial or ethnic group are not as great as they were. For me, as a child, of course, the explosion of DNA testing in recent years has also really changed the game in terms of people feeling stuck. I have a lot of friends who were just kind of stuck, and I know a lot of people who are still stuck because those things aren't perfect. That said, there are plenty of people who have found things out about their families and found their biological families that they otherwise wouldn't. In the Black community, I think there's always been an understanding of foster care and adoption on this spectrum of targeted child removal, similar to what you find in the Native community. That said, we still don't really get to talk to each other, adoptees and fosterers. There was an organization that was very active I was part of 10 to 15 years ago called Adopted and Fostered Adults of the African Diaspora, and they had a gathering in the Bay Area some years ago. And of course, we adoptees, most of us you look in the room and most of us are mixed with white, compared to those who were fostered, who were all darker skinned, not mixed. And, I mean, it was really actually life-changing because they were just like, "Look, we were just told that you all were great, that you all were fine because you were adopted, you were in permanent home. To hear now you all say, 'no, I was not okay …'" I had no idea of my racial identity and what that meant and how to solidify it and why that might be important. There was racial violence in our communities. Really, I want to highlight that word because I feel like with Reproductive Justice issues in general, these are embodied experiences, the dynamics of power that get written out on the body and get played out on the body in different groups of people, different communities' bodies. Most of us look in the room, and most of us are light-skinned mixed, right? Most of the foster folks are dark-skinned, right? These are things that, like, okay, you can know it intellectually, but when it's embodied right in front of you, oh, my God.

Bakhru: Thank you so much for that response to your word embodied. I think that's one of the things for me that's so significant about adoption and foster care and using Reproductive Justice as a framework to understand it because it's part of the whole spectrum of issues that are embodied experiences. Our embodied experience is such a fundamental part of who we are, how we walk through the world, and how we experience the world. So that's what I was thinking when you used that word. I think it's really important. The next question is, what role do you think personal memoir and fiction have in telling stories about adoption, foster care and human rights?

Gibney: I love this question because that's my wheelhouse, especially with the new book. Let me contextualize by saying I'm a mid-career writer. I am 47. I've got about three books, three to four books behind me, and I've got four books coming out in the next year.

Bakhru: As a writer, I'm just going to say that's a lot of books. Congratulations.

Gibney: I feel very fortunate to be here. People are always like, "Oh, my God, that's a lot." And then I'm like, "It is." Also, I always say I started writing when I was six. I am not talking about the quality of the writing when I was six. But I've been writing a long time, and so I'm sure you all know it's not an easy game—writing and publishing isn't an easy game at all.

Benson: Right.

Gibney: Yes, it's overwhelming. There's a ton of work; different projects are at different stages. I feel so good about it. Like I'm in that sweet spot. Like I'm doing the work I'm supposed to be doing, finally. Yes. But thank you. It's very exciting.

I should also say that there are different genres. I've got a co-authored children's picture book, actually, co-authored with another transracial adoptee called *Where We Come From*.[5] And that's coming out in October 2022. *The Girl I Am, Was, and Never Will Be* is coming out in January. I've got a single children's picture book, meaning I'm the sole author, coming out in the spring (*Sam and the Incredible African and American Food Fight*, illustrated by Charly Palmer)[6] and then in the fall, myself and Nicole Chung are editing what we believe to be the first and only anthology of short stories by adoptees with adoptee protagonists. So, yeah, so it's just like a lot of really good, timely stuff. This has been overdue; we've needed this for a while. I feel like, as a writer, you have this conscious idea of what you write about or what are the issues that you're preoccupied with. And so, what's been really interesting for me is my second novel, *Dream Country*,[7] which is about five generations of a Liberian and Liberian American family, and it takes place over 200 years and two continents. Yes. I'm always writing and investigating about race, always identity, family, belonging, and all this stuff. What's interesting is once you work on a book for a while and it's yours, it's like a baby. It goes out into the world, and it's like a child, and it's not yours anymore. It comes back to you through other people, through their experiences and their perceptions, and they're filtering through it. The connection doesn't always have to be just about adoption. I was talking about this with a dear friend of mine who immigrated with her family to the United States from India when she was eleven. She could identify with a lot of some of the questions that I'm grappling with in this new novel memoir. What the fuck is it? I don't know. In *The Girl I Am, Was, and Never Will Be*, there are two main timelines. The first timeline is my name at birth, Erin Powers, growing up with my birth mom in Utica, New York, in 1985. There's the second primary timeline, which is "what really happened," Shannon, me, growing up in Ann Arbor, Michigan in 1985. And then I'm a nerd. There's a wormhole that kind of connects the two timelines. Or we could say parallel universes, and Erin and Shannon mess with it and see each other through it at times. The more that they do, the more things that don't belong in one timeline kind of appear in the other, and things start to get botched, and it starts to get weird. So, when I was telling my friend about it, the friend who's not adopted but an immigrant, she said, "It's only been in

Benson: the past five years that I stopped imagining that there was another Shalini Gupta walking around in Delhi."

Benson: Wow.

Gibney: Yeah. I think that there are certain questions and certain Gordian Knots that cannot be inhabited or investigated only through scholarly work. I think that's particularly true for people who have these breaks—these discrete breaks. And it's usually right around trauma. There's no way that you can turn away from the fact that not only would you have had another life, a completely different life, had your mother not relinquished you, for example, but literally your entire sense of reality and your ability to describe it would be fundamentally altered, too. So, I mean, those are the things that I feel like a personal memoir, fiction, genre bending, all these things can really get at. Still and yet now, it's interesting that most of the writing by adoptees about our experiences and even about what Kimberly McKee calls the adoption industrial complex are memoirs. That can become its own trap because that can be a way to just talk about the individual and not the structural system that is operating and that creates these predetermined outcomes for individuals. I think in my twenties, I was more interested in looking at things from a structural point of view. There's also this objectification that I felt as well when people knew aspects of my story, and they'd be like, "My God, you should write about that. I want you to talk about my personal story and how fucked up it is." My response was always like, "I'm not going to fucking write about that. I'm never going to do that because I have no interest in packaging this for somebody's titillation or whatever." Even if somebody was coming from a really supportive place, that's just how I felt. That's why I think *The Girl I Am, Was, and Never Will Be* is in the form that it's in because it's like, no, I want to do both, actually. I want to talk about my personal story and like how fucked up it is that, like, "Oh, this is your birth certificate. Only it's a lie. Like, oh, this is where you were born. Oh, maybe not, because I can lie all the time, and so can international orphanages and middlemen and whatever. Oh, and also, you have no health history." Just all this stuff that's just like in the ether. You still have to live in this world, right? You still have to go back to the issue of embodiment. You have to move through this. It's not an intellectual exercise. So I have been grappling with that, I think, in the process of writing *The Girl I Am, Was, and Never Will Be,* this is a surreal experience, actually. That's also something that we would call adoptee humor. Where other people are like, "That is like the most tragic thing I've ever heard of. And why are you laughing?" And adoptees are like, "Really? Because it's fucking hilarious (in a black humor kind of way) to us."? I always go back to this very brief interaction I had with my dear friend Dr. JaeRan Kim, who is a Korean adoptee and teaches in the social work department at the University of Washington. She and I, early on in our friendship, had this exchange where I was like, "I was a steal. I think I was like $500 in 1975 from my adoption agency." She's like, "Oh no, I got you beat, like 1973, from the Korean orphanage. I was $375." And I was like, "No, bitch. Because your parents had to buy plane tickets and that is going to put you over the edge (of being more expensive). So, I was more of a deal." People listening who are not adoptees are just like horrified and were dying laughing, right? Because it's just like this is the level of absurdity that we have been put into. Through no fault of our own, at a certain point, what else can you do about that? So, I mean, I do feel like it has to be both. It can't just be a personal narrative. Nicole and I made a strategic choice for *When We Become Ours: A YA Adoptee Anthology*[8] that we weren't going to accept memoir because there's just so much memoir already, and we really wanted to challenge folks with something different. We feel like there are enough people now who are established writers and adoptees who have the chops and the training to really look imaginatively at how your imagination as an adopted writer gets translated to fiction on the page. That's what we really wanted to do. I know that's a circuitous answer. I hope I answered you.

Benson: No, it's great. I really like how you talk about speculative fiction. Not just fiction, but speculative fiction in the role that can play in kind of imaginations around rupture. It reminds me of the introduction to *Octavia's Brood*[9] when the editors wrote about how all activists are science fiction writers. Because to make a better world, you have to first imagine it.

Gibney: Yes.

Benson: Thank you for bringing that in because that adds another strand of complexity that I think is really helpful when we're thinking about these things. Our last question is kind of the big question of the book. What relationship do you see between reproductive justice frameworks and adoption foster care systems in the U.S.?

Gibney: Yeah, it's a big deal. I think one of the big problems is that people don't know what Reproductive Justice is. But it's out in the ether, right? It's everywhere. Reproductive Justice, it's just not definitely because of where Reproductive Justice comes from, the communities that it comes out of, which are historically marginalized communities of female-identified people. Black women, Native women, all this stuff. I feel like once you actually honestly look at adoption and you look at foster care both as systems and, like, I don't know what you would call them, human factories? Like factories for creating specific types of humans and particular types of kinship arrangements? There's just no way that you can actually understand what you're seeing and or experiencing if you don't have some lens of Reproductive Justice. I mean, before I had a Reproductive Justice lens, like, okay, I know the history of child removal from Black communities and communities of color. I know the disproportionate weight that Black women have to bear because of intersections of racism, sexism, and classism. And I know that abortion is just one part of bodily autonomy and definitions of freedom and kinship, being able to actually have some freedom around your kinship size, defining what they are, imagining what they could be feeling, like you have some power to enact some of the stuff. So, I mean, I feel like it's just such a powerful way, a powerful lens to put on these systems because it lays bare the power dynamic and the unequal distribution of resources How the rhetoric is just completely not aligning with what's actually going on and the effects on the most vulnerable people in the system. I went to be a U.S. social forum[10] maybe 15 years ago, and myself and some other friends who are adoptees, Korean adoptees, did a session on child removal from communities of color, and it was heartening because we weren't sure anybody was going to come, Because there was, at that time, like, no recognition. I'm like, this is a social justice issue that y'all should be aware of. It was like 20–30 people came, and they're all from different backgrounds: social workers, community activists, environmental justice workers, and everyone was just like, "Yeah, people need to be making these connections a lot. We're frustrated because we feel like we're completely siloed." I feel like that's gotten better, certainly, in the past 15 years. But there's a long way to go.

Bakhru: I appreciate you saying that because we are hoping the readers of this book will be a cross-section of people like students, but maybe also people who are involved in social work or people who are involved in nonprofits or policymaking or whatever. I think that I really appreciate what you're saying because it's like to lay that out from your perspective; I think it is helpful to the audience that will be hopefully reading the book.

Notes

1. Shannon Gibney, *See No Color* (York, Pennsylvania: Maple Press, April, 2020).
2. Gibney, *The Girl I Am, Was, and Never Will Be: A Speculative Memoir of Transracial Adoption* (New York: Dutton Books, January, 202).
3. See, Dorothy Roberts, *Shattered Bonds: The Color of Child Welfare* (New York: Basic Civitas Books, 2002); Roberts, *Torn Apart: How the Child Welfare System Destroys Black Families– and How Abolition Can Build a Safer World* (New York: Basic Books, 2022); Roberts, "I have Studied Child Protective Services for Decades. It Needs to Be Abolished," *Mother Jones*, April 5, 2022, https://www.motherjones.com/crime-justice/2022/04/abolish-child-protective-services-torn-apart-dorothy-roberts-book-excerpt/.
4. Roberts, *Shattered Bonds*.
5. John Coy, Gibney, Sun Yung Shin, Diane Wilson, Dion MBD, illus., *Where We Come From* (Minneapolis: Carolhoda Books, October, 2022).
6. Gibney and Charly Palmer, illus., *Sam and the Incredible African and American Food Fight* (Minneapolis: University of Minnesota Press, 2023).
7. Gibney, *Dream Country* (New York: Penguin Books, 2018).
8. Gibney et al., *When We Become Ours: A YA Adoptee Anthology* (New York: Harper Collins, October 2023).
9. Sheree Renee Thomas, foreword to *Octavia's Brood: Science Fiction Stories from Social Justice Movements*, Walidah Imarisha and Adrienne Maree Brown, eds. (Chico: AK Press, April, 2015).
10. The United States Social Forum is a movement making process bringing together social justice activists in the United States. The movement takes the form of an ongoing series of gatherings with the aim to create shared social justice goals and build ties between multi-racial, multi-sectoral, inter-generational, diverse, inclusive, internationalist organizations and individuals. See, https://web.archive.org/web/20110430192948/http://www.ussf2010.org/about.

2
"SYSTEMS OF CARE" IN FOSTER CARE AND ADOPTION

Foster care and adoption are processes that are deeply personal yet are played out in the lives of, and on the bodies of, individuals and families. They are not isolated, wholly individualized experiences but instead link the individual, the family, and the community to larger political bodies and financial interests. In order to fully understand foster care and adoption, we must look at them holistically and systemically. Foster care and adoption are so-called systems of "care" that draw on racist, colonialist, and neoliberal tropes about which kinds of bodies, families, and communities hold value and which do not. They are one of the many institutions, including religious institutions, state and federal governments, and corporations, that shape who and what counts as a family and normalize the rights that go along with family formation. As such, foster care and adoption systems communicate to society that families are allowed to be legible, legitimate, and fully human.

Contemporary foster care, despite its name, frequently causes more harm than the system provides care. While foster care was "once part of a broader vision of publicly provided family security, in which poverty alone would no longer force the break-up of families,"[1] the modern foster care system emerged from a larger child welfare system that excluded poor families of color and failed to offer actual security. Within the core of this phenomenon lies deeply entrenched sexist and racist ideologies about the value of reproductive labor, of Black women in particular, and women of color more generally. Because of the immense harm the child welfare system and foster care inflict on poor families of color, Dorothy Roberts argues that the term *family policing* is more accurate. She states:

[F]amily policing, like criminal law enforcement and prisons, is designed to serve the U.S. racial capitalist power structure, governed by profit, wealth accumulation, and market competition for the benefit of a wealthy white elite, by regulating and disrupting the most disenfranchised populations in place of meeting human needs. Family policing targets Black families in particular and relies on racist beliefs about Black family dysfunction to justify its terror.[2]

In the context of this chapter, we treat modern-day foster care—and often adoption as well—as a form of involuntary and forced family separation. While caring for non-biological children has taken many forms in a variety of cultures over time, forced family separation has been a tactic used throughout U.S. history to implement and maintain colonization, enslavement, and white supremacy. The current form of the foster care system is a relatively modern development that started to take its current shape in the mid-twentieth century. However, the forced separation of children from their parents is a strategy that has been used time and again by the state to further its own interests. Those interests often align with capitalist aims rooted in colonialism and racist ideologies.

Since foster care and adoption are so deeply entwined with the colonial aims of a capitalist state, we feel it is critical to examine these mechanisms of family separation through both a Reproductive Justice and Transnational Feminist lens. This chapter looks specifically at the use of forced family separation as a tool of neoliberal terrorism in the United States by connecting its practice across time and specific historical circumstances. In this chapter, we contextualize the most recent episode of "zero-tolerance" family separation during the Trump administration within the American tradition of family separation through enslavement and again by way of Indian boarding schools in the nineteenth century. By connecting these distinct but deeply entwined moments and analyzing them through the frameworks of Reproductive Justice and Transnational Feminism, we can better understand family separation and respond to the need for justice.

What Is the Family Separation Policy?

Globally, we are at a moment where we have reached an apex of neoliberalism. It is a moment, as Mohanty writes, "marked by market-based governance practices on the one hand (the privatization, commodification, and proliferation of difference) and authoritarian, national-security driven penal state practices on the other."[3] Simultaneously, as Madeleine Albright pointed out in her book, *Facism: A Warning*, authoritarianism is on the rise in Eastern Europe, North Korea, the Philippines, Turkey, Russia, and the United States.[4]

Against this backdrop, we can use the intersection of Transnational Feminism and Reproductive Justice, two different but related frameworks, as an analytical tool to formulate a response to the convergence of social, political, and economic forces unique to the current globalized era. By using these frameworks together, which were outlined in detail in Chapter One, scholars and activists can focus attention on the intersecting axes of inequality that shape family separation, foster care, and adoption in a globalized era. Looking at the example of Donald Trump's 2016 election, and his administration's family separation policy, it becomes clear that using Transnational Feminism and Reproductive Justice theories is necessary.

The election of Donald Trump is but one specific event, and scholars and pundits alike have ruminated about the causes of his ascension to political power. Canadian author and social activist Naomi Klein argues that Trump is a symbol of hyper-capitalism and the neoliberal reliance on white supremacist and sexist ideology to enact and prop up oppressive structures around the world.[5] As Naomi Klein articulates in her 2017 book, *No Is Not Enough: Resisting Trump's Shock Politics and Winning the World We Need*, for Trump, "the presidency is in fact the crowning extension of the Trump brand" and the completion of decades long efforts by proponents of neoliberalism to destroy the public sphere and create a fully corporate state.[6] She further explains that among the main pillars of Trump's political and economic project are: 1) the deconstruction of the regulatory state (such as rolling back regulations on corporations or weakening those agencies that are intended to be regulatory bodies, such as the Environmental Protection Agency); 2) a full-bore attack on the welfare state and social services rationalized in part through bellicose racial fear mongering and attacks on women for exercising their rights (this can be seen in the attempts to cut government programs for food subsidies, housing subsidies, or education); 3) the unleashing of a domestic fossil fuel frenzy that requires sweeping aside climate science and gagging large parts of the government bureaucracy; and 4) a civilizational war against immigrants in general, specifically "radical Islamic terrorism with ever-expanding domestic and foreign theaters (which can be seen in the Muslim ban or in the incarceration of thousands of migrants along the Southern U.S. border).[7] Klein's book was published in mid-2017, in the early days of the Trump presidency. As time progressed and Trump remained in office, we saw these concepts further materialize through the implementation of particularly severe social policies and practices, of which there are many examples.

One especially draconian policy was that of forced family separation when migrants entered the United States without documentation, many of whom were seeking legal protection under asylum laws. By examining Trump's family separation policy through the two lenses of Transnational Feminism and Reproductive Justice, we clarify how the related mechanics of misogyny, racism, and hyper-capitalism have produced this dehumanizing result. Working from this knowledge, we can take action in response.

The Trump administration's family separation policy were publicly acknowledged in the summer of 2018, although separations began in secret as early as the summer of 2017.[8] As journalist Caitlin Dickerson details in her exposé for *The Atlantic*, the Trump administration used family separation as a zero-tolerance approach to a perceived migration crisis along the southern border of the United States. According to her piece "An American Catastrophe," the policy began as a regional response to a popularly perceived threat in El Paso, Texas, and expanded shortly thereafter to New Mexico. More than 1,700 families were separated before the policy was publicly acknowledged. Although the government claimed that its aim was to prosecute parents who crossed the border illegally with their children, evidence shows that the separation of families was itself the goal of the policy. Evidence suggests that the policy was conceived as a means to deter so-called "illegal immigration" across the U.S. border. Dickerson quotes Attorney General Jeff Sessions warning in May 2018 that "[i]f you don't want your child to be separated, then don't bring them across the border illegally. It's not our fault that somebody does that." The use of physical separation as a deterrent makes the policy particularly harsh since often there is no real *choice* for desperate migrants who cross because they face even worse threats at home. True to that promise, families were separated, whether they entered the United States legally, by claiming asylum, or without documentation.[9] Children were removed from their parents and placed in the custody of the Office of Refugee Resettlement in shelters and facilities around the country.[10]

"An American Catastrophe" shows that between April 19, 2018 and May 31, 2018, nearly 2000 children were separated from their parents at the U.S./Mexico border.[11] Dickerson details how the U.S. government knew this policy was unpopular but deliberately lied about its practice until it was no longer possible to do so. According to her, many bureaucrats knew the policy was immoral and impractical, and they could foresee the disaster on the horizon, yet these warnings were ignored.[12] Young children were sent to so-called tender age shelters, and others were placed into the foster care system. While previous administrations, such as the Bush administration, had also practiced separating families, doing so was a consequence of a parent being charged with criminal activity. Under the Obama administration, when migrants were detained, it was done so together as a family. While there are laws that outline how children should be treated in these circumstances, none mandate the separation of children and parents.[13]

The implementation of the policy was an unmitigated disaster. There were no protocols in place for tracking children and parents, no guidelines for what to tell parents or children, and no plan for reuniting them. Dickerson relays a witness account in *The Atlantic*:

> Neris González, a Salvadoran consular worker who witnessed many of them, recalled a sea of children and parents, screaming, reaching for one another, and fighting the Border Patrol agents who were pulling them apart. Children were clinging to whatever part of their parents they could hold on to—arms, shirts, pant legs. Finally the agent would pull hard and take away the child, González said. "It was horrible. These weren't some little animals that they were wrestling over; they were human children."[14]

The 1997 Flores Agreement[15] limits how long children can be detained and requires that the government release minors to parents, guardians, or licensed facilities as quickly as possible. The 2002 Homeland Security Act is consistent with the Flores Settlement Agreement, stating that children in U.S. custody should be cared for and placed in the least restrictive facility depending on their particular needs and that children should be placed together with siblings as much as possible. Nonetheless, the Trump administration justified their family separation policies by claiming that migrants exploit regulatory loopholes while seeking to enter the United States "illegally."[16]

On June 26, 2018, District Court Judge Dana Sabraw ordered an injunction that the government should return all children under five years old to their parents. However, to date, the government has not fully complied, and to make matters worse, they have not kept accurate records, losing children in the system.[17] The American Civil Liberties Union (ACLU) notes that as of June 2019, seven children are known to have died in Custom and Border Protection detention centers.[18] The Human Rights Watch has documented that "[d]etention and family separation, even for short periods of time, have serious adverse consequences for mental well-being, particularly for those who have already suffered trauma."[19]

Parents who migrate to the United States, particularly women and asylum seekers, are fleeing violence, economic crises, and conflict that are often byproducts of the economic restructuring and social/political destabilization that is a hallmark of globalization.[20] Once in detention, they also experience neglect, sexual harassment, and assault, as well as a lack of sanitation, including lack of access to basic necessities like menstrual products.[21]

According to the ACLU, the majority of migrants originate from Central America, Guatemala, Honduras, and El Salvador.[22] More and more women and children are migrating, in addition to men, not only to escape economic instability, as noted above, but also because the costs of smugglers have increased as a result of law enforcement measures. Elizabeth Oglesby, an associate professor at the Centre for Latin American Studies at the University of Arizona in Tucson, has said, "[w]here it used to cost around $1,000 to make the journey from Central America, it now costs up to $12,000, making shuttle migration impossible. The only way for families to stay together is for women and children to migrate."[23] Under these conditions of social and economic crisis, it is women—particularly those who are most marginalized due to their immigration status, socioeconomic class, or race—who become the shock absorbers of such policies and shoulder the heaviest burdens.

In our minds, it is a natural reaction to be horrified by family separation practices. While targeting the most vulnerable people, they are inhumane and cruel. Various organizations and individuals have mobilized by filing lawsuits against the government, protesting, holding vigils, donating goods to those being detained, and so on. We suggest that, in addition to these actions, we try to understand what is happening in an intersectional, interdisciplinary, and Transnational way in order to cultivate a nuanced and in-depth understanding of the globalization forces at play in family separations.

Family Separation and Enslavement

Family separation during the Trump administration was by no means a new phenomenon. The forced removal of children and violent separation of families is a tactic that has been used repeatedly in the formation and continuation of the United States and its political and economic interests. The forced separation of families has a unique set of effects that prove highly effective as political and neocolonial tools. The policy terrorizes a community, sows the seeds of generational trauma, becomes a symbol of ideologies about both the dominating and subordinated groups, reinforces racial hierarchies, and can often result in the accumulation of material wealth for its perpetrators. As Laura Briggs points out, "The architects of the [Trump administration's] border policy are hearkening back to the racial nationalism of a country that, until at least 1865, could imagine itself as white. African, African-descended, and sometimes Indigenous people who were resident in it were held in slavery."[24] Forced family separation under enslavement was terrifying and deeply wounding; it is a mechanism used to maintain a racial hierarchy and dehumanize a population into commodities and a source of wealth for those in power.

The reasons for separating parents from children, sisters from brothers, and other family members from each other were numerous. Separation of a family member, through sale or other means, could occur due to division or sale of property upon a slaveholder's death, to settle a debt, to purchase a slave as a gift, or to mitigate personal shame or embarrassment. Regardless of the rationale, owners held absolute power in making the final decisions pertaining to the sale of enslaved people's family members. For parents losing children, there was no recourse, institution, law, or person who could stop this tragedy. Only two states, Louisiana and Alabama, mitigated family separation by regulating the age at which children could be sold away from their mothers. As Heather Andrea Williams states:

> Practices of sale and purchase varied, but for enslaved people, the single most important fact was that owners had the power to divide what they would do with the people they owned. They decided whom and when to sell. They decided which children would be sold with their mothers and which would be separated. They decided whether to keep families together or to ignore familial bonds, and their actions held great consequences for enslaved people. Every death of an owner, every auction, and every sale portended separation for the enslaved child and parents; every transaction could bring about loss and grief.[25]

Personal loss, tragedy, and trauma were not only disregarded, they were good business practice, as the forced separation of families meant the accumulation of wealth for owners and traders.

The institution of slavery produced and reinforced ideas about the inability of enslaved people to have full emotions or deep feelings of attachment to their children. Such dehumanizing notions were deeply connected to other stereotypes about Black women's sexuality, the disposability and fungibility of their bodies, and their (in)ability to feel physical pain.[26] Furthermore, regulations granting slave owners the power to consent or forbid marriage reinforced ideas about the capacity of enslaved people to have moral power and human attachment. This justified the white slave owners' views that separating families was of little significance. In fact, white people continuously bore witness to the pain and harm of family separation during enslavement as "masters, mistresses, traders, auctioneers, and purchasers."[27] While reactions of white people to family separation ranged from indifference to remorse, "money generally won out over sentiment."[28]

One can draw a direct connection to racist characterizations that carried on through the twentieth century when Black women were deemed unfit mothers, Black fathers became stereotyped as absent, and Black families were seen as dysfunctional. This racism resulted in the disproportionate removal of their children into foster care.²⁹ The image of the Mammy, in particular, continues to shape contemporary notions of Black womanhood and Black families. The Mammy, as a figure, took great care of white children under the supervision of white mistresses but was unable to competently care for the children she bore. Connecting to the present day, evidence shows that agents of the child welfare system are more likely to break up Black families than any other family.³⁰

Slavery was a racist and capitalist pursuit that answered only to the market it created, not the needs of parents, children, or families. At the same time, slavery was absolutely necessary to the political and economic interests of the state as it established itself. This unique convergence of white supremacist capitalist patriarchy marks forced family separation. Enslaved people were viewed as valuable commodities for their unpaid labor in harvesting tobacco, cotton, rice, sugarcane and for the development of the colonized land itself. The language of slavery was the commodified language of the market: property, warranties, mortgages, deeds, valuables, stock, and inventories.³¹ Slavery also had the effect of commodifying sexual violence and rape since slave children were assets to accumulate, regardless of how they were conceived.³²

It is important to note that throughout the period of enslavement and after, separated family members continued to remember loved ones and frequently searched for them while bearing the pain of separation. In her work, *Help Me to Find My People*, Heather Andrea Williams details the depth of emotion, resilience, courage, determination, and creativity of those who were forcibly separated from loved ones and their efforts to reunite.³³ Her research demonstrates that the system of slavery, which relied so heavily on the breaking apart of families for economic and political gain, and which transformed people into commodities, could not fully extinguish their humanity.

Family Separation and Indian Boarding Schools

Similar to the forced separation of families during enslavement, the United States government embraced family separation as a strategy in its dealings with Native Americans. As a newly established national government and settler state, the future of the United States was dependent on the subjugation and dislocation of Native Americans and the colonization of Native American land. "According to prevailing republican theory, only a society built upon the broad foundation of private property could guarantee public morality, political independence, and social stability."³⁴ The pursuit of this aim took a multipronged approach and included broken treaties, war, genocide, enslavement, and settlement of land, to name just a few. Characterizing Indigenous people as savages, devoid of civilization, and less human than white settlers was crucial to the white supremacist capitalist agenda. Within this context, Indian Boarding Schools became an essential tool to the United States' project of nation building.

The nineteenth century saw the rise of the off-reservation Indian boarding schools whereby the U.S. government separated Native children from their families and relocated them to residential schools with the intent of "civilizing" them through assimilation and acculturation. The process of civilization "included a commitment to the values of individualism, industry, and private property; [and] the acceptance of Christian doctrine and morality, including the 'Christian ideal of the family.'"[35] This act was part of a larger strategy to strip Native children of their language and culture and to establish white economic, political, and social dominance. The 1819 Civilization Fund Act provided religious organizations the funds to run schools for the purpose of "introducing among them the habits and arts of civilization."[36] The first off-reservation school, the Carlisle Indian School, opened in Pennsylvania in 1879.[37] Its founder, Captain Richard Henry Pratt, drew on his experience overseeing Native prisoners at Fort Marion in Florida for the running of the school. He is known for infamously stating that the key to civilizing Indians was to "kill the Indian and save the man."[38] The off-reservation boarding school model was deemed so successful at the task of acculturation that it became the model for many other schools across the country.[39]

In reality, Indian boarding schools were not sites of education but sites of trauma and loss. Children were separated from their parents and community. Brothers and sisters were separated since boys and girls were kept apart. Even older and younger siblings of the same gender were often separated. Native language and Native dress were prohibited, as was the practice of any cultural traditions, including singing, praying, dancing, or art.[40] In most cases, students were not provided an education and were instead subjected to manual labor and strict military-style discipline and uniformity.

The Meriam Report (Lewis Meriam, 1928) provides a description of the boarding schools in which "investigators found children living in overcrowded dormitories, sometimes without even adequate toilet facilities, subject to appalling health conditions, ill clad, ill fed, and ill housed."[41] Over a century later, Meriam's description of the ill-treatment of separated Native children is strikingly similar to the experience of children separated from family at the U.S./Mexico border. As Laura Briggs states in *Taking Children*, "The doctrine that created boarding schools was cited by the second Bush, Obama, and Trump administrations to justify not only detention centers, but the whole conduct of the 'War on Terror'—insisting that it is exempt from judicial review because of the plenary power doctrine, which gives the executive branch unfettered power over Indian matters."[42]

The forced separation of Native children was crucial to the white supremacist and capitalist goals of an emerging nation state. Specifically, family separation was a tool for the dispossession of Native land and the enrichment of white settlers. White power over the lives of Native children undermined tribal self-determination and thereby made Native lands vulnerable to the extraction of natural resources, robbing future generations of resulting profits. It also facilitated forced cultural assimilation and genocide, ensuring white dominance.

Child separation was critical for the implementation of many other Indian policies. The trauma and dislocation that child separation caused were vital to undermining tribal authority, the theft of land, and the crushing of language and culture. Native studies scholar Dr. Soma de Bourbon points out that the violence of family separation toward Native and Black women and their children can be understood

> in part, as an investment in the state and white American property interest that denies Native American women, parents, and communities of reproductive autonomy. [T]he removal of Native children from their mothers and communities [is] an act of reproductive violence linked to slavery. [Currently] Native children are the most overrepresented ethnic group in foster care and state-assisted adoption (Wildeman and Emanuel 2014), with the highest racial disproportionality index of any group (Rosay 2016). The removal of 25–35 percent of Native children from their families is simultaneously a violation of an Indigenous people's reproductive rights, a group-based harm against the community, and an investment in whiteness. The state-sanctioned infusion of whiteness with property interests over Native women's reproductive freedom through the termination of parental rights and divestiture of children is tied to their historical entrapment in state-sanctioned systems of slavery.[43]

In this way, the bodily and reproductive violence that Indigenous women experienced (and continue to experience) not only denied their individual and community reproductive autonomy but also propped up social and economic hierarchies that privilege whiteness and hyper-capitalism. We must acknowledge this legacy of reproductive injustice in the formation of the United States.

Connecting the Dots

Similar to the misogyny, racism, and hyper-capitalism that worked together and fueled the separation of Native families to residential schools and the sale of enslaved Africans away from their kin, the pursuit of U.S. state and corporate interests drove the Trump administration's zero-tolerance policy. In fact, we can trace the history of U.S. government interventions in Central America as a means to prop up U.S. economic interests abroad and connect it to the recent family separation policy.

The majority of migrants who experienced family separation under the Trump administration started their journey from Central America, particularly Guatemala, Honduras, and El Salvador. They were fleeing violence and political and economic instability. These instabilities were created, or at least seriously exacerbated by, the U.S. government intervention in those emerging democracies as a means to protect U.S. corporate interests. As Julian Borger stated, "[e]xperts on the region argue, however, that when politicians or activists have come forward on behalf of its dispossessed, the U.S. has consistently intervened on the side of the powerful and wealthy to help crush them, or looked the other way when they have been slaughtered."[44] For example, in the northern Guatemala highlands, small-scale farmers were being forced off their land to make space for agribusiness in sugar and biofuel. The domination of agribusiness in Guatemala can be traced back to the 1950s and the coup, backed by the United States, against the democratically elected president Jacobo Arbenz. At the time, Arbenz had tried to seize certain areas of land from the U.S.-owned United Fruit Company and distribute the land back to Guatemalan farmers. The U.S. CIA backed the Guatemalan military, which committed genocide against the Indigenous population, resulting in the rise of new military dictatorships and destabilizing the country.[45]

Similar stories can be seen in El Salvador, where the U.S. government spent nearly four billion dollars supporting the Salvadoran military to fight left-wing revolutionaries during their civil war, and in Honduras, which was used as a staging area for American intervention in Nicaragua in the 1980s.[46] As Leandra Hinojosa Hernandez states in "Feminist Approaches to Border Studies and Gender Violence: Family Separation as Reproductive Injustice," "an analysis of [the] intertwining of geopolitical, geospatial, and colonialist actions illustrates how institutional, societal, and political structures across borders caused political unrest and economic collapse that necessitated the quest to find asylum."[47] There are deep connections between the pursuit of U.S. state and corporate interests, the displacement of people, and the resulting strategy of family separation to justify the racist and misogynistic actions and outcomes of those very pursuits.

To make the situation even more egregious, the recent family separation of migrants from Central America to the United States has become a billion-dollar industry built on the backs of women and children. Over the past ten years, the child detention industry has increased tenfold.[48] As the Associated Press reported, "Health and Human Services grants for shelters, foster care, and other child welfare services for detained, unaccompanied, and separated children soared from $74.5 million in 2007 to $958 million in 2017. The agency is also reviewing a new round of proposals amid a growing effort by the White House to keep immigrant children in government custody [indefinitely]."[49] Costs include tents for housing, beds, food, foster care, medical and psychological services, transportation, and so-called "secure care," which is code for employing guards. Recipients of government funds include nonprofits, religious organizations, and for-profit entities. Some of the largest amounts of funds for detaining children have gone to Southwest Key and Baptist Child and Family Services, which received a 1.39 billion dollar grant to operate shelters, and GEO Group and Core-Civic, both of which are private prison companies and have contracts to run the lion's share of Immigration Customs Enforcement (ICE), detention facilities.[50] These last two companies alone, both of which donated heavily to the Trump campaign, earned a combined $985 million from ICE contracts.[51] In short, there is money to be made and wealth to be accumulated through the separation of children from their parents and family members from each other. All of these organizations function as government contractors to the Department of Health and Human Services, although they are more a function of a militarized approach to dealing with a social issue than anything else. In this way, the conflation of corporatization and militarization that Transnational feminists has long pointed out becomes clear as it gets played out on the bodies of asylum-seeking migrants.

The result of what we have just described is a reinforcing system where state interventions are used to prop up U.S. corporate and state economic interests, which in turn creates political, social, and economic instability, leading to an increase in racialized and gender-based violence. These circumstances, along with economic push and pull factors, become a catalyst for families to migrate. Those families are then placed in privately run detention facilities from which those same U.S. economic interests profit. As Hernandez puts it, this system

> cages families; it traumatizes children and exposes them to mental and physical risks; and it erodes the central family unit in efforts to defend and protect the 'sovereignty' of the United States. The U.S. government under the Trump administration is enacting legal policies to sanction family separation and maternal/child abuse while simultaneously

evading acknowledgment of its hand in spearheading wars throughout Latin America that necessitated the need for asylum seeking in the first place.[52]

In this way, family separation during the Trump administration joins family separation of enslaved Africans and family separation of Indian boarding schools as a mechanism for advancing U.S. imperialism vis a vis the reproductive capacity of childbearing people.

Conclusion

There is a reason family separation is addressed in multiple human rights documents, including the United Nations Universal Declaration of Human Rights; the United Nations Convention on the Rights of the Child; the Convention Concerning the Powers of Authorities; and the Law Applicable in Respect of the Protection of Infants, the International Covenant on Civil and Political Rights.[53] Family separation is also addressed in the Convention on the Prevention and Punishment of the Crime of Genocide.[54] The forced separation of families strikes at the heart of the right to security and control over one's body and to be free from coercion or violence. It undermines the ability of individuals and communities to uphold their right to self-determination and be principal actors and decision-makers in their reproductive lives.[55]

This chapter demonstrates that in order to fully understand foster care and adoption systems in the present, we must look to the past and see how control over the reproductive potential of Black, Indigenous, and people of color is central to the formation of the United States itself. Our hope is that the reader can see the threads that connect racism, sexism, and globalization. These threads create a web that links seemingly disparate people across place and time, and it exposes the mechanics that prop up global capitalism at the expense of people with childbearing capacity, their children, and their communities who are deemed less valuable. We can't see something like the family separation policy in a vacuum. We must constantly historicize and contextualize in keeping with the hallmark of Transnational Feminist frameworks. Family separation is part of a legacy of domination and exploitation that uses people's reproductive capacity to destroy families and communities, and it simultaneously maintains a gender, race, and economic hierarchy. It happens time and again in various geographic and temporal spaces.

By using Reproductive Justice and Transnational Feminist frameworks to understand these examples, we suggest there is a need to think critically about foster care and adoption as it is presented in subsequent chapters. Recognizing connections across time and space, national boundaries, and various identity categories is vital to building the solidarities necessary to create a more equitable world. How can we understand the lived reproductive and sexual experiences of gender and sexual minorities, especially women, in seemingly contrasting social and geographic places and build alliances between individuals and communities? Seeing these connections is vital to creating solidarities and alliances amongst and between groups working for change.

Notes

1 Catherine E. Nymph, *Raising Government Children* (Chapel Hill: University of North Carolina Press, 2017), 8.
2 Dorothy Roberts, *Torn Apart: How the Child Welfare System Destroys Black Families– and How Abilition Can Build a Safer World* (New York: Basic Books, 2022), 27: emphasis added.
3 Mohanty, *Feminism Without Borders*, 970.
4 Madeleine Albright, *Facism: A Warning* (New York: HarperCollins, 2018).
5 Naomi Klein, *No Is Not Enough: Resisting Trump's Shock Politics and Winning the World We Need* (Chicago, Haymarket Books, 2017).
6 Klein, *No is Not Enough*, 5.
7 Klein, *No is Not Enough*, 5.
8 Caitlin Dickerson, "An American catastrophe: The secret history of the U.S. Government's family-separation policy," *The Atlantic*, September, 2022, https://www.theatlantic.com/magazine/archive/2022/09/trump-administration-family-separation-policy-immigration/670604/.
9 Dickerson, "An American Catastrophe."
10 John Burnett, "What happens when parents and children are separated at the U.S.-Mexico border," NPR, May 30, 2018, https://www.npr.org/2018/05/30/615585043/what-happens-when-parents-and-children-are-separated-at-the-u-s-mexico-border.
11 Dickerson, "An American Catastrophe."
12 Richa Nagar and Amanda L. Swarr, "Theorizing transnational feminist praxis," in *Critical Transnational Feminist Praxis*, Swarr and Nagar, eds. (New York: State University of New York Press, 2010), 1–20.
13 Dickerson, "An American Catastrophe."
14 Dickerson, "An American Catastrophe."
15 "Flores *v*. Reno Settlement Agreement," was a stipulated settlement in the case of *Flores v. Reno*, 507 U.S. 292 (1993), filed August 12, commonly referred to as the "The Flores Agreement."
16 Maya Rhodan, "Here are the facts about president Trump's family separation policy," *Time*, June 18, 2018, https://time.com/5314769/family-separation-policy-donald-trump/.
17 Cynthia Pompa, "Immigrant kids keep dying in CBP Detention Centers, and DHS won't take accountability," American Civil Liberties Union, accessed June 24, 2019, https://www.aclu.org/news/immigrants-rights/immigrant-kids-keep-dying-cbp-detention.
18 Pompa, "Immigrant kids keep dying."
19 Human Rights Watch, "In the freezer: Abusive conditions for women and children in U.S. immigration holding cells," Human Rights Watch, accessed February 28, 2018, https://www.hrw.org/report/2018/02/28/freezer/abusive-conditions-women-and-children-us-immigration-holding-cells.

20 Amanda Baran and Sameera Hafiz, "Trump's first 100 Days: Immigrant women and families on the frontlines," We Belong Together, accessed 2017, https://webelongtogether.org/sites/default/files/WBT100days_report.pdf.
21 Baran and Hafiz, "Trump's first 100 days."
22 "Family separation: By the numbers," ACLU, October 2, 2018, https://www.aclu.org/issues/family-separation.
23 Julian Borger, "Fleeing a hell the U.S. helped create: Why central American journey north," *The Guardian*, December 19, 2018, https://www.theguardian.com/us-news/2018/dec/19/central-america-migrants-us-foreign-policy.
24 Laura Briggs, *Reproductive Justice: A New Vision for the 21st Century*, vol. 2, *How All Politics Became Reproductive Politics: From Welfare Reform to Foreclosure to Trump* (Oakland: University of California Press, 2017), 17.
25 Heather Andrea Williams, *Help Me Find My People: The African American Search for Family Lost in Slavery* (Chapel Hill: The University of North Carolina Press, 2016), 37.
26 C. Riley Snorton, *Black on Both Sides: A Racial History of Trans Identity* (Minneapolis: University of Minnesota Press, 2017).
27 Williams, *Help Me Find My People*, 91.
28 Williams, *Help Me Find My People*, 97.
29 Dorothy Roberts, *Shattered Bonds: The Color of Child Welfare* (New York: Basic Civitas Books, 2002).
30 Roberts, *Shattered Bonds*, 60–62.
31 Williams, *Help Me Find My People*, 38.
32 Laura Briggs, *Taking Children: A History of American Terror* (Oakland: University of California Press, 2021).
33 Williams, *Help Me Find My People*.
34 David Wallace Adams, *Education for Extinction: American Indians and the Boarding School Experience, 1875–1928* (Lawrence: University Press of Kansas, 1995), 18.
35 Adams, *Education for Extinction*, 7.
36 Harmeet Kaur, "Actually, the US has a long history of separating families," CNN.com, accessed June 24, 2018, https://www.cnn.com/2018/06/24/us/us-long-history-of-separating-families-trnd/index.html.
37 Kaur, "History of separating families."
38 Kaur, "History of separating families."
39 Margaret L. Archuleta, *Away From Home: American Indian Boarding School Experiences, 1879–2000*, Margaret L. Archuleta, Brenda J. Child, and Tsianina Lomawaima, eds. (Pheonix: The Heard Museum, 2000).
40 Archuleta, *Away From Home*.
41 Lewis Meriam, "The problem of Indian administration: Report of a survey made at the request of Honorable Hubert Work, Secretary of the Interior, and Submitted to Him, February 21, 1928," (Baltimore: Johns Hopkins Press, 1928), quoted in Laura Briggs, *Taking Children*, 57.
42 Laura Briggs, *Taking Children*, 46.
43 Soma de Bourbon, "White property interests in native women's reproductive freedom: Slavery to transracial adoption," in *Reproductive Justice and Sexual Rights: Transnational Perspectives,*" ed. Tanya S. Bakhru (New York: Routledge, May 2019), 15–32.
44 Borger, "Fleeing a hell."
45 Borger, "Fleeing a hell."
46 Borger, "Fleeing a hell."

47 Leandra Hinojosa Hernández, "Feminist approaches to border studies and gender violence: Family separation as reproductive injustice," *Women's Studies in Communication* 42, no. 2 (June 2019): 130, https://doi.org/10.1080/07491409.2019.1605213, 130.
48 Martha Mendoza and Larry Fenn, "Detaining immigrant kids is now a billion dollar industry," AP News, Associated Press, July 13, 2018, https://apnews.com/article/wa-state-wire-az-state-wire-mi-state-wire-ct-state-wire-tx-state-wire-289b015df6e94ac6b2a35c28b11365b5.
49 Mendoza and Fenn, "Detaining immigrant kids."
50 Mendoza and Fenn, "Detaining immigrant kids."
51 Mendoza and Fenn, "Detaining immigrant kids."
52 Hernández, "Feminist approaches to border studies," 132.
53 Sonja Star and Lea Brilmayer, "Family separation as a violation of international law," *Berkeley Journal of International Law* 21, no. 2 (August 2003): DOI 10.15779/Z388350.
54 Star and Brilmayer, "Family separation."
55 Sonia Corrêa and Rosalind Petchesky, "Reproductive and sexual rights: A feminist perspective, *Physis Revista de Saúde Coletiva* 6 (December 1995): 147–177, DOI 10.1590/S0103-73311996000100008.

WRESTLING WITH COLONIAL LEGACIES OF IÑUPIAQ FAMILY SEPARATION

Interlude with Roo Ramos

Roo Ramos is an Iñupiaq, Two Spirit, liberation and equity consultant with over 20 years of experience in the nonprofit sector and advocacy, activism, and systems change work. They work to help organizations, businesses, and government agencies to decolonize and truly integrate the full spectrum of equity in their work. Roo spent much of their career advocating for Indigenous children, youth, and families in the school, justice, healthcare, and foster care system. They are able to advocate and organize in those spaces because of their lived experience. They are passionate about building communities where these systems are no longer required. They have a bachelor's degree in journalism with a minor in Native American Studies and an MBA in healthcare management. Roo is passionate about helping organizations create safer, more inclusive spaces for their employees, board members, and clients. Their progressive executive-level experience has been a key factor in helping to create and facilitate executive management support that leads to real change. They are on a journey to reclaim and learn the Iñupiaq language and hope to someday write children and teen books in Iñupiaq. They own Redfox Consulting, and they are the staff-chosen Executive Director of Spectrum Center in Spokane. They also run the Indigenous horse program at the Urban Native Youth Organization and are a board member of Sila, an Iñupiaq-led cultural and environmental preservation organization based in Alaska.

Tanya Bakhru: Thank you so much for sharing your time and your knowledge with us. I'm very excited about this book project and the voices of the folks that we are interviewing to bridge that gap between theory and practice and make it really accessible for all different kinds of readers. So thank you again for making the time. The first question is just to get us started, which is: what brought you to the work that you do now?

Roo (Qallaq) Ramos: I'm a product of the systems in which the inequities are so deeply rooted in colonialism and imperialism. And I am a half Indigenous person whose mom was caught up in the courts and who got sent to the Good Shepherd Home here in Spokane, Washington. That's how I ended up in Spokane. My family's from Kiana, Alaska. My grandmother is Iñupiaq, and that iterative, colonial, violent process led me to be in existence in Spokane, Washington, where my mom had no support and where the systems were targeting poor brown people and limiting their children. Luckily, I was born after 1978, [when] the Indian Child Welfare Act (ICWA)1 was in place, so I was not allowed to be adopted out of the community, and I think it literally saved my life. ICWA saved me from being adopted by white parents. That would have led me to being in a totally different world, and my mom probably would have died. I can pretty much say that I saved my mom so many times. I think she would have died had I not been present, and my mom is one of the most glorious human beings I know, [even] as sick as she was in terms of mental health. She called the CPS on herself to protect us. And you know, as much as that felt like a betrayal, it was also an act of radical love for her children that she was able to do that. The system itself broke my spirit more than any of the trauma I experienced at the hands of my mom.

When I was twelve years old, I was in a foster home; they had legal custody of me. They had legal guardianship over me, and they were abusive on every level. They treated me like I was a slave. I was raising their biologically born child at that point. He was three years old when I was just turning thirteen. So he was two-and-a-half to three years old when I ran away, and I was his only primary caregiver.

He called me mom. Not because he didn't understand that my foster mom was his mom but because he associated "Mom" with me as the primary caregiver. When I left, I had to make a decision. I had to decide if I was going to continue to let these systems make decisions for me, and I was no longer willing to do that. I was no longer willing to give up my own humanity to satisfy the needs of a system that didn't give a shit about me.

That's when I found my voice; I had just turned thirteen years old. I walked into Crosswalk, which is a homeless youth shelter. I walked in, and I saw the director, who my mom knew because she volunteered every year. My mom may not have been able to work and may not have been able to do a lot of things, but she knew about giving back to her community. My mom knew the executive director, and he knew her as well. As soon as I walked in the doors, he knew who I was. I'd been running away for two weeks, and I was like, "Okay, it's time to officially get back into my mom's life." And I walked in, and I found my voice. He called the CPS worker. We sat down, and we had a discussion, and I said, "My intention is within the next year to be reunited with my mother. If that is not your intention, you will have trouble on your hands everywhere. If you take me, I will run away every time you do something. I will make it hard for you. So you have a choice. Put me in a foster home temporarily, with the intention of reuniting with my mom by the end of the year." He said that wasn't possible. I said, "It *is* possible, and you're going to make it happen. I don't care what you do. I don't care what the system says. The system separated me from my mom. They can undo it. I'm not stupid." And that's how I spoke to my caseworker, who I thought was abusive and neglectful. Nine months later, I moved in with my mom.

That's when I decided I was no longer going to just stand by and watch these systems cause harm either to me or to other youth. That started my career. I'm autistic, is what I've learned, and I am queer as fuck, and I didn't belong anywhere. I held myself back from being myself. When you're in foster care, you learn not to have a personality, not to have an opinion, not to do anything, and that's what I did. I learned to mask my existence and my humanity in order to be successful in getting my needs met as a child. So that's what led to me being an advocate for racial equity, being an advocate for calling out imperialism and how capitalism is the worst economic structure in the fucking world, and why I care so deeply about protecting, particularly Indigenous children. Hence, [that's] why I helped rewrite the Indian Child Welfare Act (ICWA) for Washington State,[1] and that's why I'm an executive director of the Spectrum Center[2] now and why I have a business that is pushing systems to do better, even if it's part of the nonprofit industrial complex. I still believe that nonprofits are the place where we can really impact systems and push systems.

Bakhru:
Krista Benson: Thank you so much for sharing all of that with us.
I have a follow-up question because I'd like to hear a little bit more about it. So, could you tell us what revisions you were a part of making to the Revised Code of Washington (RCW) for the ICWA in Washington?[3] I know that it was revised, but can you explain what needed to happen? And also, if you thought there were any limitations to that process, as you experienced it?

Ramos: Yeah, they pulled out all the teeth in the RCW. I was invited to participate because I'm a product of ICWA. At the time, I was working at the Native Project,[4] doing a lot of the ICWA programming for Indian children in the region [who were] involved in the system. I was positioned well to advocate and to testify and to edit and revise what was written. There are a couple of things we really focused on like redefining what "active efforts" are. So, not just visitation with Mom, but actually trying to get the parents or biological family to be in a place to be able to take care of the child in a real way. The other thing that we really were trying to focus on was redefining the idea of a caregiver because the system itself is iterative. What happens is you get one family getting reported to child protection, and then they get an open case. There is some validity to it, so they are in the system for a brief amount of time. And then, ten years later, the grandmother needs to protect their grandchild. This happened in the case of my biological niece, who is my daughter. Since that parent had an open case back in the day, now they're no longer eligible to take on those children, right? The ultimate point of the system is to end Indigenous parenting of Indigenous children, and that's how they make it work right there. The hope in rewriting ICWA for Washington was to redefine it to get a little more specific, to really push on what we consider parental and kin involvement. I was pushing for potential charges, or financial repercussions, for failing to meet those standards for caseworkers and for supervisors—That, of course, got completely eradicated.

Benson: Any time people have tried to put any kind of consequences into ICWA, as far as I know, at both the state and national level, it's been taken out.

Ramos: You can just see the line. I was thinking about it because I've done a lot of growth in the last six years, and what I've come to realize is that previously, I was so reactive to talking about my foster care experience. I've been in foster homes, and I know how abusive they are and how clinical they are. How institutionalized they are. They're not homes. And I never once felt safe, I never once felt like I belonged, I never once felt like I could just be me, not one fucking foster home, not one. It's so interesting to be forty-one years old and see support in place for those aging out of the system. I'm not saying we shouldn't have those in place, but why are there nonprofits doing the work that caseworkers and foster parents should be doing? They're being paid to do it. Why do you have to have a teen clothing closet for foster kids? Because I know how much money you're getting.

Bakhru: It's nonsensical. It's nonsensical because it is not designed to make sense.

Benson: Exactly. Why are you paying foster parents to take care of these children when you could just pay the parents?

Ramos: The system operates the way it was designed to, which is to steal brown children from brown families so that white parents can continue to live their dreams of having their 2.5 kids and their white picket fence. That's it. There is another thing about foster care that really is really fucked up: You're forced to go to therapy, with or without parents, sometimes with your siblings. Every foster sibling and every foster kid I've ever talked to has a negative experience with the mental health system because it's never actually addressing the trauma that we're experiencing. It only specifically talks about the trauma with your biological parents, which, oftentimes, like with my mom, I didn't have that. My mom loved us. My mom was able to love us in very, very real ways. To make me talk about the trauma with my mom because she drank occasionally, she smoked, you know, she sacrificed her own health so that we were fed and we were loved, and we had Christmas, and we had birthdays. I always felt that love that people talk about having with their mom. I have that. My mom is super sick. My mom has dissociative identity disorder, my mom has anorexia, my mom has BPD [bipolar disorder]. We're talking [about] severe, severe mental health issues. Despite that, my mom was the most loving human I've ever met. To this day, I take care of her, and I will take care of her to the end of her days, or the end of mine, because she taught me how to love, and she never destroyed that trust. So when you go to counseling, and they're like, "Let's talk about your abusive mom," and we're like, "My mom wasn't abusive ever…"

Benson: The therapist isn't set up to be able to talk about the trauma of being removed from your mom, or your family being under-resourced, or the fact that we don't have a social safety net for people experiencing really intense mental health issues. It's a lot easier to ask you to do some cognitive behavioral therapy around something that wasn't actually the problem.

Ramos: I remember being five years old and doing a one-on-one or a family session with my mom and my brother and [me], and then my mom was leaving. We were going to our foster home. She was going to go home, and I remember I hated that foster home. I remember the feeling; I remember everything in my body telling me that I was not safe in that foster home and that I needed my mom. My mom was the only safe person in my world besides my brother, and I remember holding onto her and refusing to let go and telling them, "I'm not doing this today. Not going to let my mom go. I'm not; we're not doing this today." And I remember holding on to her, and I was at Spokane Mental Health, which is now Frontier Behavioral Health.[5] I remember four adults grabbing me and my mom to separate us, and I refused to let go. I was a little monkey because I was like teeny tiny, and it took about ten minutes of them trying to separate us because I was so intensely not willing to let go. They finally threatened my mom. They said, "If you do not convince her to let you go, you will not have visitation for a month." I was like, "Well, I can't miss out on my visitation, so fuck that shit." I let go.

But instead of addressing the trauma of being separated from my mom, the focus was always on what my mom did or didn't do. And I was like, "You all are confused." I was thirty-nine when I started therapy—like, active therapy. I've chosen the therapist, I've chosen the pathway, and I'm giving permission to the process. That's the first time I've ever done that.

Benson: You weren't given the opportunity to choose those things before.

Ramos: I had such a bad taste in my mouth. I felt like I could never trust a therapist. Now, I trust a therapist. Did you testify about how abusive the system was? No, you testified to thinking it was about my mom.

Bakhru: Is there anything else you'd like to speak to in terms of the relationship between foster care and historical and intergenerational trauma in Indigenous communities? This is both about how this

	system replicates itself and also any other kind of connections that you see.
Ramos:	The colonial mindset doesn't allow for Indigenous parenting. There are no moral or ethical codes that are respected in Indigenous parenting that are comparable to the way the white people do it, so we're always being accused of something. I am a professional. I am an executive director of a non-profit. I have been in this community for fucking thirty years, my whole life, and in the last year and a half, CPS has been called on my family twice. So what I'm saying is [that] it doesn't matter. I have a master's degree; I'm learning my Indigenous language. I own my own business. I am the executive director of an organization and a well-established, well-loved organization in this town, and they still are calling the CPS on us.

My son was at a friend's house. They snuck out. They got drunk, like teenage boys do. We were called at 10 a.m. to "Come get your son. He needs medical attention. Come pick up your son. His face is bloody." We took him to the Urgent Care. They immediately grill us as if we are the reasons why he has a bloody nose, and I don't think white people have those same experiences. We literally left thinking that we will never go back. That's CHAS,[6] a huge organization in this town. It serves 100,000 patients. It is the community health facility here. So, everybody who has Medicaid, Medicare, all of those who are low income, they're all going to CHAS, and they called CPS on us twice in the last year and a half.

We went to go get an ADHD assessment a month ago. We told our son, "Hey, you already are getting your mental health meds from them; they 're already on a plan. You've been regularly going to the doctor for your mental health medication." We are asking for an ADHD assessment. They called, and they grilled him. They actually asked to speak to him alone. We were like, "Why did you say yes?" I think he learned his lesson. Then they pushed him to admit that he had done some self-harming and had some suicidal ideation. I am not really sure how the conversation went, but they brought my husband |

back in. Our son came out and was like, "They're trying to call the cops on me too. They're trying to get me into the mental health ward."

This is how bad it is. The people who had to do the well-child check with my son when he got hurt they knew who I was. They met me, and they're like, "Oh you do racial equity training and Indian Child Welfare training? I know you." My husband was like, "And you're still... What?"

For me, it's a cycle of violence. It's a continuation of the eradication of our existence. All [CPS] is for Indian children or Native children, Indigenous children, is a way to continue the assimilation and the destruction of our humanity, our culture, and our ways of being. It is nothing more than that. It is not saving our children. It is not protecting our families. It is not keeping us united. It is the exact opposite. It is the weapon of choice for the American government against Indigenous people.

Bakhru: What would restorative justice look like for Native communities around histories of family separation?

Ramos: There is nothing. There's nothing they can fucking do to make right what they took from us. What they took from me. I say destroy the fucking system and start over. Literally, destroy it all. Burn it down. Maybe decide that capitalism and imperialism are actually the root evil of all. Until we focus on connection, humanity, love for ourselves and our neighbor, seeking out joy, and deciding that we're no longer here to be a fucking cog of economic growth and GDP, it doesn't matter what they do. They're keeping us down through this system, and this is just for those who happen to get away. Indigenous people keep on getting away, so they keep on trying to steal us. They keep on trying to make us into shells of our humanity so that we agree to our own destruction, and I'm not willing to participate in that. There is no way to make right what happened to my mom. The stories that my mom could tell if you wanted to talk to somebody about the other side of the foster care system, or the residential school system, of how our own people take in that violence and decide to replicate it because they have no other way to achieve safety. My mom could tell you stories upon stories. I've always wanted to write a book about my mama because my mom could tell you what it's like to be the victim of imperialism and colonialism at the hands of her own mother. My Iñupiaq name is Qallaq. It's my grandmother's name. I carry it because she died before I was born, [and] I think it is my tie and to my grandmother's Spirit. Why else would I have ended up the way I have but to make right what my grandmother's Spirit failed at doing, which is being a good mother, being an Indigenous mother, one with love and support for her children. She stuck a gun in my mom's vagina and threatened to kill her. She would take the iron and put it on your leg. You can see the scar to this day. My mom has dissociative identity disorder. Since I was in high school, I have bought Christmas and birthday gifts for a five-year-old little girl inside my mama. She comes out, and she's so scared.

There's nothing that can be done to make this right, and I carry this with me physically, mentally, spiritually. I had to have mechanical menopause because I was so sick from endometriosis. Come to find out, I am autistic. I don't need a fucking white system to tell me that I'm autistic. I know I'm autistic, and along with that comes potential for other comorbidities. I haven't been officially diagnosed. I have a doctor's appointment in June. I think I've got Ehlers-Danlos Syndrome,[7] and I think they could have found out about it when I was a child when I was in the system. You want to talk about medical neglect?

Do you know that I was at the Shriner?[8] My mom took me to the Shriner's Hospital when I was seventeen or sixteen years old because I had such bad sprained ankles that I couldn't walk. I sprained my ankles every other week. Ehlers-Danlos Syndrome is a syndrome that causes you to not have very good cartilage. It's literally a systemic issue. I wonder, what if I had been diagnosed properly when I was a child? I was eight or nine years old when they diagnosed me with malformed feet. The big toe grew out, and then I got this huge bunion, and I couldn't walk. They never got me proper footwear, and you're supposed to have proper footwear. This is Ehlers-Danlos Syndrome, and I wonder what my life could have been like if I had been properly given the medical attention. I went years without going to the doctor when I was in those foster homes.

And now I have no children of my own. I will never be able to have my own children. They took that from me. The other thing when I was thinking about reproductive justice is, can we talk about sexual abuse? Can we talk about the fact that I was so lost and so alone? When I was in high school, my mom was very, very ill. I was her nurse. She was too sick and weighed eighty-four pounds. I was alone. I had no one. My white dad was abusive and didn't give two shits about me. I went to an Indigenous school, and I met a teacher there. And that teacher groomed me and started a relationship with me. He was more than thirty-two years older.

It's taken me all these years to finally be starting to talk about how I wasn't consenting. I was a fucking victim. I took SafeSport training for my horse show. That's how I knew what grooming was, know what I mean? Everybody's talking about grooming, but I never applied it to myself until I started reading. [SafeSport is] from the gymnastics abuse scandal.[9]

Now, every Olympic sports confederation/organization, every single athlete, has to take that. That's when I realized that I had been groomed by an Indigenous man. It was the week before I turned seventeen when I met him. I told myself, "Well, you knew what you were doing. You were practically an adult," and I held myself responsible for that relationship this whole time. And now I'm like, if my child were to start a relationship at almost twenty years old with a forty-nine-year-old man, I would flip my shit. I would go hunt him down and threaten to cut off his scrotum if [he] came near my child again; that's the real truth.

It was never my fault, and Indigenous people in this fucking town, who knew about it, who were on my local Indian Child Welfare Act committee when I was a child, did not report it. They knew. Toni Lodge fucking knew, Pam Austin ... These are the aunties of the Indigenous Community here in Spokane. They knew. We're so sick that we were performing the violence on each other.

Bakhru: I want to talk about the abolitionist movement and about organizations that are trying to create something different and trying to create something new. From your perspective, what would that look like? What are the things that are needed? What are the elements of something that we can create that actually supports people? I really appreciate the points that you're making about connection and about humanity. What are the things that we need to honor people's humanity to fortify those connections?

Ramos: I think leaning into love and leaning into our base human construct that is connection, that is relational, and that is shared liberation. It can only happen if we can admit that capitalism, imperialism, and colonialism are the problem.

I don't think we can change how we do business officially until that happens because we have to sign a new social contract with each other. I hear all this talk about how we can't open up talking about the Constitution. Everybody's like, "We don't want to open those can of worms." I'm sorry! What Indigenous person signed that social contract? What Black person signed that social contract?

What, any number of brown cultures signed on to that? Tell me one, just one. Now, tell me, one woman? There ain't no woman either. Who the fuck signed that contract for us? A bunch of landowning slave-owning sexual deviants? That's who the fuck signed those contracts for us, so it ain't right until we make it right. Sure, I'm going to go and "Vote Blue," and I'm gonna do all the things, but the real truth is until we are truly ready to lean into radical love, radical connection. If you are leaning into those things, then you inherently know that you have to redo the Constitution. The Constitution is not protecting me. It's not protecting you.

Bakhru: When you're talking about radical love and interdependency, it made me think that there could have been a situation where your mom wouldn't have been alone. It would have yielded a situation where she would have had support in a variety of ways—financially, emotionally, and healthwise. The move to talk about individual failures is really an excuse to hide the way systems of forced family separation are built to fail people.

Ramos: Yes. My mom was fully capable of providing us a loving home, and they still chose to remove us. She wasn't abusing us. She wasn't even neglecting us. She wouldn't meet the standard of removal.

They would have said, "You have an alcohol problem. Let's provide you with some treatment." What would they do with active efforts, right? I don't know what would be my experience right now had my mom been provided with resources. They misdiagnosed her for many, many years. That's part of the problem, right? The mental health system is so colonial that it can't imagine how to see a whole person.

A whole person, a whole Indigenous person. If you can't see that, you can't perceive my mom. My mom's autistic. How am I autistic if I don't have a parent who is somehow on the spectrum, right? Ehlers-Danlos syndrome is inherited. It's a recessive gene, a double recessive gene. My parents had to have it for me to have it. What support did my mom miss out on having? I'm telling you, my mom is autistic. It is so clear to me that my mom is autistic. She's not very verbal, to be really honest. My mom can barely speak to and hold whole conversations with people outside of my family because she cannot talk to people.

I think about her learning. She was never a good student. She really struggled in school; she's not capable of understanding nuance in the same way that other people are. The system failed my mom on more than one measure and then, in so doing, failed me and my brother on every measure, too. My brother is in prison, [and] was in prison for all of his daughter's first ten years of life, essentially,

This is why, at this point, it's like there's nothing this system can do to make it, right?

It would start on the way [toward justice] if we were to say every foster child in this fucking town, in this fucking world, gets five acres somewhere.

Let's even get back to reparations—a little bit of reparations for every foster child, every Black person, every Indigenous person—let's do that. Let's remove the lands from the corporations and give it back to the people who they've stolen it from and who they're still trying to steal it from. They're trying to prevent people from having a choice in their freaking lives about what happens to their bodies and what happens to their future. We're just supposed to sit here and just pop out babies — that you again steal from us, right? That's what they're doing. That's what they want. Why? There are white parents out here who can't have babies, and that's what they've always done. The ultimate success of this system is the removal of Indigenous, Black, and brown children and placing them into white families. Who wants the cute little brown baby? Oh, my cute little pup. Oh yeah, he's part of Inupiaq. That's what they wanted to do with me. My mom told me that when I was a child, she said, "Baby, they're going to try to take you. They want a cute little baby like you." I tried to stop being cute. I was a little odd in my way of doing it, but I tried. I did.

Benson: Is there anything else you think we should know? Are there other strands you want brought in here? Is there anything else you just really want to make sure you have a chance to say here?

Ramos: I'm very triggered by foster parents, and I need foster parents to understand why. Foster parents think that they can provide a home that my parent could not, and yet, they fail so miserably, over and over and over again. They were demanding that I call them mom, eradicating my own mother in my own brain. Demanding that I perform or behave in such a way when you haven't even told me that is an expectation. Not having a negotiation with a child whose very life has just flipped upside down. You can't even find out from me what I need. What is important to me to feel safe? What spatial issues do I have? What food? What safety do I need? How do you just take in a child, fit them into your family and think that they're going to feel like they belong? Do you even know me? These foster parents don't care about knowing your style. I got taken from my mom before ICWA came into play, and I got placed with my mom, even with my mom's past history with the foster care system, so that's the situation I was trying to explain.

And when they finally were like, "Okay, you know Tara—my name at the time was Tara—is the stable person who is going to be providing for the whole family," and that's why they were able to get around my mom. But my mom provided the most childcare. I was working! How else was I providing for the family unless my mom was doing childcare? My mom is a fucking amazing childcare provider. I think what bothers me is that my daughter did go for two months, she lived with a foster family up north. When we went to visit her, when it happened, they took her from our home and placed her in a foster home. We said, "This is her favorite pillow," and it was a handmade satin red pillow that [my daughter] Scyla liked the touch of because my kid is also autistic, so she needed that to feel safe. Like, that's her. That's her thing.

They lost it. The one thing that she needed, the one thing we expressed to the foster parents. I think my mom texted them. I think I texted them the importance of that pillow, and now she describes how she used to force herself to touch the things that cost her the most harm. Have you ever seen *The Accountant*?[10] It's a good autism movie. If you want to understand me, it's a really great choice. Ben Affleck, his character is autistic, [and] he's the accountant. His dad forced him to learn how to fight in order to manage his autism. Every single day, at exactly the same time, he puts on music as loud as he can. He puts on the lights that flash, and then he rubs something on himself. He's forcing himself to be exposed to the things that caused him problems and harm. Scyla describes that now, and I think it's connected to her loss of the thing that was soothing to her. That's the kind of shit that the system can do to us. And no one cares. No one cares that she lost her most precious item. I had a similar item called my Jinx. It's my blanket; my mom made it for me when I was five, and I've never lost it. It has been with me my whole entire life. It's an Afghan, Jinx is its name, and I've had it in every foster home. But I was older. Scyla was two-and-a-half years old when she went into the foster home. She couldn't advocate for herself. She could barely speak, right?

Benson: I really think that you have a powerful voice as someone who has been in the foster care system, let alone someone who's had multiple generations of family members in the system and who was failed by the system. That's certainly the most common story I hear when I talk to folks who experienced the foster care system. I don't hear a lot of happy fucking stories, you know?

Ramos: We need scholarly investigations into the impacts of these systems because they're not doing the review. The education system is similar. My friend, Dr. Timothy San Pedro,[11] wrote a book about decolonizing or how Indigenous mothers build indigeneity in their children. This is important to me, too. I'm a product of this system. I'm an iteration of myself, a version of myself, in this timeline that has been completely, and so wrenchingly, impacted.

With no care for my humanity or health, or my happiness, or any interest in seeing that I'm successful — How many foster kids have a master's degree? Your own system is failing to produce good citizens. In Washington state, foster kids who age out of foster care are supposed to be receiving free college education. It's not true in all states, but that is true in Washington. Even then, the numbers of foster kids with degrees are not great, [and] we need to talk about that. Why did I succeed and other foster children didn't? I can tell you it's deeply rooted in the fact that when I was thirteen years old, I found my

Benson: fucking voice, and ain't nobody going to take it from me, and by God, I was going to make it out alive, and I was going to change the world for my family. I wasn't going to stand by and keep being targeted.

Benson: What touches me is that the onus shouldn't be on a single thirteen year old to do it. It's so amazing and profound that you had that realization, and then you had the fortitude to do everything that you've done in your life, but that shouldn't have been on you to do that, right? We shouldn't have to rely on an individual thirteen-year-old person to have this realization in order to …

Ramos: Save her family.

Benson: Yeah. I really appreciate the points that you're raising about the basic community because that's where the Reproductive Justice framework is very useful. It really makes us have to talk about and reimagine what it means to care about each other. What does it mean to acknowledge our own humanity and the humanity of other people? And what does that actually look like in real terms? Sometimes, it might mean things like providing free college tuition, but in a deeper sense, that means reconstructing the whole notion of care and community in the first place. That is what I hear you saying, and I really just am very much taking that to heart.

Ramos: The people who benefit from this system the most are the ones farthest from their own humanity. That's why they can't imagine my mom's humanity and my humanity, and my brother's humanity, and even my children. The rest of my children's humanity is not valued and understood. The majority of people who are actors in these systems have to have a social contract in which they let that go, [and] they probably lost [that humanity]. Most of them, unless they're Black, brown, queer, trans, or some alternative lifestyle, probably already signed away their own souls in order to continue benefiting from the system. Our job these days is to try to figure out how to get white cishet men to value themselves enough ultimately. I know that sounds crazy, but that's the real truth.

Bakhru:	Because if you can't see your own humanity, how can you see someone else's?
Ramos:	Yeah.

Notes

1 Washington State Indian Welfare Act, Revised Code of Washington (RCW) 13.38.010 (2011).
2 Spectrum Center, Spokane, Washington. See: https://www.spectrumcenterspokane.org. Spectrum Center does advocacy, activism, and community building in eastern Washington and North Idaho.
3 The Revised Code of Washington (RCW) is the compilation of all permanent laws currently in force in the state of Washington. The Washington State Indian Welfare Act was added to the RCW in 2011. It provides that tribes be notified and allowed to intercede in child custody matters. These state laws must be written in accordance with the federal Indian Child Welfare Act of 1978.
4 The Native Project, https://nativeproject.org/, "provides medical, dental, behavioral health, pharmacy, patient care coordination, wellness, and prevention services for both Natives and Non-Natives in the Spokane community," See: https://nativeproject.org/about-us/
5 Frontier Behavioral Health is a nonprofit that provides behavioral healthcare and related services in collaboration with community partners in Spokane, Washington. See: https://fbhwa.org/
6 Community Health Association of Spokane (CHAS) is a non-profit, federally qualified health center (FQHC) that provides comprehensive health services in Spokane Washington. See: https://chas.org/about-chas/
7 Ehlers-Danlos Syndrome (EDS) is a group of hereditary connective tissue disorders that present as skin hyperplasticity, hypermobility of joints, atrophic scarring, and easy bruising.
8 Shriner Hospital for Children Spokane, see https://www.shrinerchildrens.org/en/locations/spokane.
9 The United States Center for SafeSport is an American nonprofit organization established in 2017 to protect young victims from sexual abuse in sport. It resulted from years of controversy over mishandled sexual abuse in youth gymnastics and the passing of Protecting Young Victims from Sexual Abuse and Safe Sport Authorization Act of 2017. SafeSport education for youth athletes is composed of three individual lessons on sexual misconduct, mandatory reporting, and emotional and physical misconduct.
10 *The Accountant*, directed by Gavin O'Connor, featuring Ben Affleck and Anna Kendrick (Warner Bros. Pictures, 2016).
11 Dr. Timothy San Pedro, *Protecting the Promise: Indigenous Education Between Mothers and Their Children*, (New York City: Teachers College Press, April 2, 2021).

3
TRANSNATIONAL ADOPTION AND INDIGENOUS SOVEREIGNTY

Introduction

Large-scale transracial and transnational adoption in the United States began in the 1950s due to a combination of different U.S. policy decisions and transnational geopolitical circumstances. Though it may seem easy to disconnect international and domestic adoption, when we analyze this history through the lens of race and citizenship, it is clear that both forms of adoption are deeply intertwined for children of color, Indigenous children, and white adoptive parents. As Kim Park Nelson explains:

> The first recorded Korean transnational adoption took place in 1953, just five years after the first American domestic transracial adoption of an African American child to a white family. In 1958, just five years after Korean transnational adoption began, the Indian Adoption Project began as a national program with the goal of placing American Indian children in white American homes. Clearly, American domestic transracial adoption as a formal practice barely predates the start of Korean transnational adoption.[1]

The relationship between American domestic transracial adoption of children of color, adoption of Indigenous children (both transracial and transnational due to Indigenous sovereignty), and adoption of Korean infants into white U.S. homes all illustrate the relationship between militarism, globalizing capitalism, and adoption as a form of family formation.

The 1950s were a time of massive change in the United States due to economic and social changes following the end of World War II and

DOI: 10.4324/9781003303442-5

the Korean War. In both wars, U.S. citizens saw themselves as "saving" children in other countries, and that narrative expanded to include transnational adoptions following both wars. After World War II, the United States saw an influx of Greek, Japanese, and Italian children, and within ten years of the end of the Korean War, Korea became the largest sending country for transnational adoption.[2] For nearly forty years, Korea remained the top sending country for transnational adoption to the United States until 1995, when Russia and China took the top spots.[3] The fact that transnational adoption in the United States in the twentieth century were always tied up with war shows one way that transnational transracial adoption has always been connected to the military-industrial complex, and highlighting these relationships was part of the reason that Critical Adoption Studies scholar Kimberly McKee coined the term "transnational adoption industrial complex." Many adult adoptees and Critical Adoption Studies scholars have pointed to these relationships as part of the process to challenge the framing of adoption as an act of child-saving, which we explore more in this chapter.

This time period not only saw an increase in U.S. militarism and its impacts but also the increased use of adoption as a form of family formation in the United States. The United States Children's Bureau estimated that 17,000 adoptions were contracted in the United States in 1937. By 1945, 50,000 children were adopted and in 1955, 91,000.[4] These numbers only increased through the 1970s and 1980s. As noted in the previous quote from Kim Park Nelson, as adoptions increased, so did the use of transnational transracial adoption, mostly into white U.S. families.

The placement of children of color and Indigenous children[5] in the homes of white U.S. citizens since the mid-1950s has both supported and helped to justify a limited view of who can be a "good" parent for children. When those making decisions about who can be a good parent understand a limited range of what good parenting can look like, as informed by white supremacist settler colonial capitalism, then the homes that contain "good parents" are going to skew toward those of white, heteronormative, U.S. citizens who are middle or upper-middle-class, the exact populations that adopted most of these children. When these assumptions happen in concert with the legal interests of "best interests of the child," people of color and Indigenous people disproportionately find themselves judged as not "good" parents and that the best interest of their children is to have them removed and placed with white adoptive families.[6]

In this chapter, we aim to draw attention to the relationship between the adoption of Korean children into the United States and the Indian Adoption

Project as sponsored by the U.S. federal government in the twenty-first century. While the adoption of Korean infants and children from South Korea into the United States and the organized removal of Indigenous children from their families and sovereign nation environments have geographic and political differences, they have striking similarities around both projects' relationships to militarism, colonialism, and racialized capitalism.

As mentioned in the introduction to this book, we were pleasantly surprised by the 2023 decision in *Haaland v. Brakeen*, which upheld the constitutionality of the Indian Child Welfare Act (ICWA) of 1978. The crux of the decision in *Haaland* centered around the decision that ICWA's preferences for Indigenous families for Indigenous children in foster care or adoption do *not* discriminate against the Indigenous children due to race. The history of ICWA's authorization—as well as the structural and rhetorical similarities between advocacy for the adoption of Indigenous and Korean children into mostly white families in the United States—shows why the framework of race is limited if it is the only framework in the analysis of the adoption of both groups of children. It is by looking at the parallels in the structures, rhetoric, and impacts of these projects that we can see that the only appropriate way to understand the adoption of Indigenous children into white U.S.ian families is both transnational and transracial adoption, similar to adoptions of Korean children.

Foundations of the Indian Adoption Project and the Korean Adoption Project

As Park Nelson points out above, it is a mistake to separate the adoptions of South Korean children into the United States in mostly white homes from the foundations of other kinds of popularization of transnational and transracial adoption more broadly in the United States. The impact of Korean children adopted into U.S. homes has profoundly shaped adoption practices in the United States, which is one reason why there has been a proliferation of scholarship on Korean adoption within the Critical Adoption Studies literature.[7] Though a comprehensive history of Korean transnational adoption is not only beyond the scope of this chapter but is, in fact, an entire field, it is important to understand the different ways that Korean adoption interfaced with U.S. social, legal, and cultural systems. Park Nelson further elucidates this history when she writes:

> The practice of Korean transnational adoption has a history of more than fifty years that includes multiple overlapping layers. One history is specific to the aftermath of the Korean War and subsequent U.S.-South Korean geopolitical relations. Another is the history of racialization of

Korean adoptees as Asian Americans, and as a part of an ongoing history of American transracial adoption. Yet another is the history of U.S. immigration policy which, for Korean adoptees, has swung to extremes. And finally, there is also the history of Korean adoptee communities themselves.[8]

Some of the points that connect histories of Korean adoption into the United States with transnational transracial adoption more broadly and Indigenous adoption specifically is the ways that both Korean and Indigenous adoptees' integration into white American families were impacted by anti-Black racism, called into question simple narratives of immigration and citizenship, and show clearly the ways that some children were desirable for white American families and others—especially Black children—were considered un-integratable. Growing awareness of these issues has led to a broader understanding of transnational and transracial adoption, including both the adoption of Korean children and Indigenous children into white U.S. homes, "as an industry, premised on the finding of children for parents, versus parents for children."[9] While this has not always been accepted, historical records make it clear that it has always been the case.

The initial rise of Korean children adopted into the United States were often children of U.S. veterans and Korean women after the Korean War. In the International Social Service (ISS) adoption records, most of these children were mixed-race children, usually fathered either by Black or white American soldiers, as we explore later in this chapter. These children were sometimes adopted by their biological fathers and their wives in the United States, but at other times, they were "suggested" by soldiers stationed in Korea to friends and family in the United States. Many of these soldiers were also adoptive parents of Korean children, such as the family referenced in a 1956 letter from a potential adoptive mother to Susan T. Petties, then-assistant director of ISS. The potential adoptive father's brother and wife had adopted a Korean child while he was serving in Korea. In the letter written to Petties, the potential adoptive mother writes that she was writing on behalf of herself and her husband, who wished "to apply for an immediate home study with regard to adopting a mixed-blood Korean orphan. My brother-in-law, who is presently stationed in Korea, has found a child of around two years of age [...]"[10] ISS approved a home study in Connecticut, where the couple lived. This adoption was approved after that home study, despite the written note by the social services professional, after a discussion with the parents:

> I feel very strongly ... [that the father] is certainly ready for a Korean child. Just how strong are [mother's] doubts is hard to say, as I am sure

her first preference to adopt an American child, but on the other hand, I do have confidence in her ability to care for a youngster who did come from Korea. I think she, more than he, is aware that there might possibly be some community repercussions, particularly when the little girl was dating age, but on the other hand, she is not too fearful around this.[11]

This one case is not an outlier when it comes to the early adoption of South Korean children to the United States. In fact, collaboration between orphanages in Korea, ISS, and social services professionals in the United States provided a template for other transnational transracial adoptions. Noting personal racism was quickly dismissed as uncommon in other reports from home studies. It seems to us that no matter how unprepared white American adoptive parents might have been to help children understand Asian American racialization in the United States, the social services professionals were similarly ill-prepared.

The end of the Korean War and U.S. occupation in Korea did not diminish the number of children being adopted by U.S. parents until well into the 1990s. Subsequent waves of adoptions, instead of being explicitly tied to American militarism and military personnel, were shaped by post-war Korean social and legal norms, including poverty and stigma attached to being unmarried mothers. Here, the post-war impacts of adoption relocating "undesirable" children—whether because of their mixed-race status or the marriage status of their mothers—facilitated further adoption mobility for decades, predicting these adoption practices on a combination of nation-building, imperialism, capitalism, misogyny, and racism.[12]

These impulses shaped the adoption of Indigenous children in the United States at the same time. As explored in the previous chapter, education was one of the first removal systems of Indigenous children in the U.S. When that program began to wane in the mid-20th century, the U.S. state turned to foster care and adoption for the same goal. The increasing numbers of Native children in the foster care system available for adoption, as well as changing U.S. government attitudes toward the use of extra-tribal adoption as a solution for poverty in Indian Country, provided an ideal groundwork for the establishment of an official project encouraging the adoption of Native children into white homes. In partnership with the private non-profit Child Welfare League of America (CWLA), the Bureau of Indian Affairs (BIA) launched the Indian Adoption Project (IAP) in 1958. Established in 1920, CWLA is a child welfare advocacy organization that aims to make vulnerable children a priority in the United States through the development and dissemination of best practices for child welfare.[13] Joseph Reid, then-Director of the CWLA, announced the pilot of the Indian Adoption Project on April 1, 1959, in a memo to CWLA member child welfare agencies. Fifty Native children, mostly from western and southwestern tribes, were to be placed with non-Native families throughout the country, mostly on the East Coast.[14] Reid predicted that many of the agencies would express interest in being included in the project. He also clarified that limited funding meant that CWLA was only able to work with the two or three member agencies already contracted with CWLA to place the Native children for the first three years of the project. He noted that there were more Native children who could be included in the project:

> We do know, however, that there are Indian children, legally free for adoption and considered adoptable, who are living in foster family care and children's institutions throughout the country because there are no adoptive homes for them. Some of these children are the direct responsibility of the Bureau of Indian Affairs and are supervised by the Indian Bureau social workers on the reservations, while other children, living off the reservations, are the responsibility of the respective state welfare department.[15]

This statement highlights both the complex legal situations of Native children in foster care—some in state care, some supervised by the BIA—and child welfare officials' understandings of Native children's adoptions as an act of child-saving. As a result, the CWLA spread the idea of white families as a better alternative to Native families. This changes the perspectives and practices of social workers outside of the project, which makes it possible for Native children's adoptions to spread beyond the formal project.

The First Decades of the Indian Adoption Project and Korean Adoption Project

Both projects encouraged white U.S. families to adopt children from South Korea and Indigenous communities. This was not their only commonality. In both cases, adoption was seen as a potential solution for a host of "social ills" that the U.S. government—and, in the case of Korean children, the South Korean government—saw as rooted in inadequate family structures and support for the children. In neither case were more resources allocated to those families of origin, nor were connected structural issues such as social judgment of single mothers, lack of financial support for impoverished parents, nor the impacts of imperialism and war on these communities addressed.

Instead, the most consistent solution offered was for children to be moved to "better" (read: white) families in the United States.

In addition, these projects were also deeply invested in capital accumulation and ensuring the wealth of the corporate state. At first, this involved only the U.S. state, though the South Korean government also became invested in the "industry" of adoption quite quickly. In both cases, the children available for adoption became the most important commodities in the adoption industry, but other parts of the industry also became important to both states. From adoption fees paid to adoption agencies to travel fees to adopt children or visit homeplaces of origin to the entire industry of adoption reunion in South Korea, adoption functioned and continues to function as a system of wealth production for both nations.

The rhetoric of child welfare officials shows the inconsistency of their ability to identify who, exactly, they are serving. Many reports and even promotional materials about the IAP and the national Adoption Resource Exchange Network of America (ARENA), developed in the mid-1960s, appear consistent with the CWLA's mission to improve outcomes for children—and thus, serve children first—when they discuss Native children "languishing" in foster care or impoverished conditions on reservations. For example, in the CWLA's report, "Indian Adoption Project," they say:

> children who may have been firmly established in secure homes at an early age through
> adoption, have been passed from family to family on a reservation or have spent years at public expense in federal boarding schools or in foster care. They have never had the security of family life to promote their development and assure their future.[16]

The CWLA rhetoric supports the idea that their primary interest is in serving the interests of at-risk youth.

Throughout IAP documents, CWLA employees and child welfare agency employees continue to reference Native children as "languishing" in foster care and note inadequate resources on reservations to provide for Native children. In a document advertising the Indian Adoption Project, the CWLA presents Native children as frequently in need of adoptive placement. The pamphlet explains:

> Illegitimacy among Indian peoples is frequently acceptable and the extended family is by no means extinct. The unwed mother may bring her child home to be cared for by herself, her family, or some relative, and he may be successfully absorbed by the tribe. However, there are many situations where this is not the case and the children are left uncared for.[17]

Even when acknowledging that Native people may have extensive family care networks, this advertising assumes that, in "many cases," this would not be accurate. Additionally, though CWLA and BIA materials frequently reference unwed mothers as targets for the removal of children, Reid himself acknowledges that many Indigenous communities and nations did not have the same stigma surrounding childbearing outside of marriage as many settler white communities had at the time.

Outside of Indigenous communities, single motherhood itself could be grounds for alleging neglect of a child[18] and may have been the justification for taking these Native children from their families in the first place. Social stigma around single motherhood also absolutely drove living parents in South Korea to "surrender" their children to orphanages, making them adoptable.

However, child welfare service agencies' interest in serving white adoptive parents is clear when CWLA officials discuss the numbers of white families willing to adopt Native children. In a 1967 report about the IAP and its successes, the writers note that in 1965, "the Project had from fifty to sixty-five approved adoptive families on referral, with far fewer children referred."[19] In this framing, it becomes more explicit that adoption agencies and the BIA often saw Native children as a supply that should meet the demand of potential white adoptive parents. This is in direct conflict with Zirtha Turitz's 1965 presentation on developing philosophy and best practices in adoption the same year, where she stated that "[a]n adoption service should not have as its main purpose to find children for families."[20] Indeed, the rhetoric of the CWLA itself contradicts this in multiple places.

Specifically, this emerged in multiple reports on the progress of IAP, including in a 1968 report of IAP accomplishments and recommendations, which reported that one accomplishment of the project was the increased social services for unmarried Native birth mothers, including maternity houses. The report claims:

> Many unmarried mothers prefer to live in maternity homes awaiting the birth of their children, rather than stay with their own families or relatives on a reservation. As adoption opportunities have become increasingly available, unmarried mothers have been more willing to release their children for adoption, knowing that adoption may afford the child greater opportunity for a better life.[21]

The assumption that Native mothers would be better off separated from their families and home communities during pregnancy is related to the assumption that the best life for a Native child is with a white family. Here, advocates blend rhetoric of the interests of the child with that of the interests of the adoptive parents so that life with the adoptive parents becomes the obvious best interest of the child. This life is a "better life" than they could ever have with a presumed- impoverished and unmarried Native mother. The Native mother's future is never mentioned in this document, as she is a figure only for the production of the adoptable child.

The IAP and its investment in the placement of Native children in white homes operated out of the continued misplaced attitude of white benevolence combined with the assumption that white families would provide a "better future" for Native children. This can be seen in the previously cited report, referencing that Indigenous mothers could know "adoption may afford the child greater opportunity for a better life." These beliefs connect all the way back to the assumption of the inadequate Native family, which justified compulsory education processes.

Kinship in the era of the IAP, however, ceases to be something that Native children could learn or unlearn, and it instead becomes a mechanism of assimilation and elimination of indigeneity. Though the IAP did not necessarily facilitate the adoption of large numbers of Native children, its impact on cultural understandings of Native children's care, the "selling" of Native children as particularly adoptable and attractive to white families, and the conclusion of child removal as the solution to Native poverty had long-ranging impacts on individual adoptees and their families for decades to come. These changed understandings of Native children's care also show shifts in understanding of childhood and shifts away from thinking of Native children as potential labor for white families, as was common in "outing programs" sponsored by many Indian boarding schools in the late nineteenth and early twentieth century.[22]

Post-1960s Rhetorics of Race and Elisions of Nationality and Sovereignty

Though the statistics and transits of Native children are pretty transparent early in the IAP, it is complicated to track youth adopted through the IAP after 1968. At this point, CWLA folded the IAP into the newly established ARENA, which was developed to address the more than sixty thousand children who would spend their lives in temporary foster homes and institutions.

ARENA's primary objective was to "find homes for children, particularly for children of minority groups, or of mixed racial background."[23] ARENA was initially funded by grants from the American Contract Bridge and Fields Foundation, individual donors, and funds from the BIA. Many of the ARENA projects focused on racialized populations. Often, promotional materials and reports cite the IAP as a model for other programs to adopt children of color into white homes:

> A successful program for American Indian children that closely approximates a national adoption exchange [for adoption of children of color] has been operated by the [CWLA] with the cooperation of the U.S. Bureau of Indian Affairs. In the past seven years, it has been responsible for the adoptive placement of 225 American Indian children with families in the 19 states—mostly White families from the East.[24]

Here, we see the IAP cited as a model program for the adoption of youth of color, a move away from understanding Indigenous sovereignty that instead classifies Native children as a racial category. This is an important part of the U.S. state's continued undermining of Indigenous sovereignty in the interests of the prosperity of the corporate state.

Early on in the IAP, CWLA officials considered Native youth a distinct population that needed to have tailored practices for their adoption, due to both citizenship status and race.

However, the establishment of ARENA with the support of the BIA illustrates one way that Native youth became classified as "minority" youth in the late 1960s. Native children's adoption was no longer tied to *other* forms of transnational adoption, such as that of Korean children, and was instead cited as an example of successful transracial adoption, eliding both Indigenous sovereignty and the transnational nature of adoption of Indigenous children into non-Indigenous families.

Yet, the adoption of Native children by white families was a very particular form of transracial adoption. David Fanshel noted in his assessment of the IAP's effectiveness that this may actually make Native children more appealing as potential adoptees for white families. He explains:

> For some people, the Indians are regarded with unabashed admiration as truly the 'first Americans' or the only 'real' Americans. The Indian is the indigenous American rather than one who has his roots on foreign shores. Not an insignificant number of Americans express pride in having some Indian background in their family histories, however remote.[25]

Adoptive parents and CWLA officials frame the acceptance of Native children into white homes in a particular understanding of Native racialization that contrasts sharply with other forms of American racialization. This is unlike Black Americans, for example, with a history of racialization steeped in "one-drop" rules, where any presence of Black ancestry marks one as

Black. In contrast, the popular understanding of Indigeneity is something that is racially distillable and—in terms of popular settler imagination—only counts if you are "one quarter" or above. This understanding of Indigeneity as distillable is due to popular misperceptions of blood quantum regulations for Native people to be enrolled as members of federally or state-recognized tribes.[26]

The idea that both Korean and Indigenous children were particularly appealing to white families was based on fraught anti-Black racism, which encouraged white adoptive parents to consider Asian and Indigenous children as more easily integrated into a white family. As Kazuyo Kubo explains, at the time, "[t]he common discourse that is engendered ... is that the racial division between white and [B]lack is too wide to cross, in contrast to the differences between whites and Asians." [27]In the case of Black children, white parents found them less "appealing" because it was assumed that "[c]hildren of African descent cannot cross racial lines. As long as the idea of race continues in America, [B]lack children will grow up to be [B]lack adults, no matter who raises them or where."[28] The adoptability of Korean and Indigenous children was partially reliant on American and Korean anti-Black racism.

In the historical records about Korean adoption, many of the reports speak to a child's "attractiveness," or, even more honestly, about the color of their skin as a proxy for attractiveness. In one 1968 report submitted to ISS by Sidney Talisman, after a visit to Korea to visit orphanages and social services organizations, Talisman writes frequently about the attractiveness of various children and how that impacts their adoptability to U.S. families. Talisman reports that:

> [o]ne prominent social welfare leader, Mr. Kim, director of the Korean National Red Cross, raised the following question. Since inter-country adoptions tend to drain off the most attractive and intelligent children, by pursuing inter-country adoption as a goal for racially- mixed children we are depleting that particular group of exactly those members who might in the future help to alter their image in the society to mitigate against prejudicial attitudes toward them.[29]

The assumption here, of course, is that Mr. Kim is referring to mixed-race Korean children who have one white parent, not those whose non-Korean parents are, for example, Black. This is evidenced across the ISS records where only Black—or, in their records, "Negro"— parents were considered to adopt children of Black and Korean descent. In the same report by Talisman, the writer notes a feature of mixed-race Korean children's transracial and transnational adoption: "Even more remarkable, these children have not come to families of the same mixed backgrounds. The Korean-Caucasian children have been placed with Caucasian Americans, and the Korean-Negro children with Negro Americans."[30] It is notable that the children who Mr. Kim seems to believe could address the social stigma of being mixed race in Korea, in this example, are likely fair-skinned and/or of mixed white and Korean heritage.

This kind of rhetoric around the "benefits" for Korean children in the United States to have at least one white biological parent did not end in the 1950s or the 1960s. In a report written in 1971, Wells C. Klein wrote a recommendation to Talisman that they develop a form that can be used in lieu of a complete home study for adoptive parents. In his encouragement, he wrote: "It is important to start on these immediately. I suggest we fill out forms for the oldest home studies first. There is a shortage of Caucasian Korean (mixed-race) children, so that flexibility should be indicated where parents have a first preference for a Caucasian Korean child, but would accept a full Korean child."[31] Here, U.S. racial systems consider not only the attractiveness of a child to potential adoptive parents but also explicitly mixed-race children are preferred, as long as their non-Korean parent is white. This racist preference for light-colored skin shows up not only in mixed-race adoptions from Korea but also in how Indigenous children were often "marketed" to potential adoptive parents, including the common practice of lightening their skin in photos.[32]

Indigenous children's navigation of these specific iterations of colorism and racism were, and remain, impacted by the complexities of Indigenous sovereignty and the ways that claims of belonging work in Indigenous communities, in contrast with the U.S. state. Ideas of biological inheritance, scientific testing for that inheritance, and use of blood quantum or DNA testing—Western ideas—are central to how people can articulate or prove themselves as Native to the U.S. state. As Kim TallBear notes, "The category of Native American DNA ties Native American history, tribal identity, and ideas of race to molecular concepts."[33] Blood quantum, the percentage of Native American heritage or "blood" that one can prove, is a complex matter for tribes and a form of member validation encouraged by the U.S. federal government because the government wanted to limit the number of "domestic dependent nations" and their numbers.[34] Along with Native adult adoptees,[35] we argue that Native children were more attractive as adoptees in part because of this dominant understanding of the ability to "eliminate" Indigeneity, tied with white U.S. popular imagination that "we are all a little bit Native." The white parents of Native children Fanshel references do not actually see themselves as Native but rather see nebulous "Native ancestry" as being a fundamentally white American attribute. We argue that this stance actually made and continues to make

Native children more appealing to white adoptive parents, as the racialization that marks Indigenous children "racially different" could be bred out in a few generations. If Indigeneity is read as race and also as racially distillable, then the Indigenous cultural and social differences could be seen as distillable, as well.

Within Indian Country, advocates of transnational and transracial adoptions of Native children recognized that, while many white adoptive families were eager to adopt Indigenous children, many Native families were becoming increasingly resistant to having white families adopt their children. Fanshel framed this resistance in understandings of race when he explained that "the increased self-pride and the changing attitudes of minority ethnic groups may well lead to increasingly vehement pressure against the release of their children to white parents. The loss of a people's children may be seen as the ultimate indignity to endure."[36] Child welfare officials seemed able to both recognize this indignity and still manage to prioritize the needs and desires of prospective white adoptive families. Later, in his report, Fanshel acknowledged that the desires of the Native families and nations should be the most important factor considered in transracial adoption of Native children: "It seems clear that the fate of most Indians is tied to the struggle for Indian people in the United States for survival and social justice. Their ultimate salvation rests upon the success of that struggle [...] Only Indian people have the right to determine whether their children can be placed in white homes."[37] It is remarkable that the director of CWLA could simultaneously recognize this and still continue to manage a project that actively sought to place Native children in white homes. This remained possible and logical due to the historical association that Native children would have a better life in white homes. Additionally, this language also suggests that if Native parents were sufficiently responsible for their children and responsive to child welfare agencies, then there would not be a need for adoption.

Who Is Adoptable? Indigenous and Korean Children in White Families

At the beginning of the IAP, administrators and social workers usually discussed Indigenous youth's tribal affiliations as a racial category, and they recognized the need to specifically deal with tribal nations and the BIA, which emphasizes tribal sovereignty. However, as the project continued, officials started to conflate Native children with other children of color or "minorities" and discussed Native youth as one possible solution for the large numbers of prospective white adoptive families not finding children. In 1965, Zirtha Turitz, the Director of Standards Development for the CWLA, presented at a regional CWLA conference on the potential use of foster placement to increase the numbers of "nonwhite children" for adoption.[38] Turitz claimed that "no child should be denied the opportunity to have a permanent family of his own by reason of his age, religion, race."[39] Children of color, including Native children, were seen as a solution for childless white families who wanted to adopt children and were finding the adoption of a white child challenging or too time-consuming. Administrators justified changing practices of adoption to potential adoptive families by referring to them as loving and as having the ability to save vulnerable children. Turitz commented:

> There is a growing body of agency experience in placing children for adoption in families of different ethnic backgrounds: the CWLA Indian Adoption Project, ISS placement of Korean children, PAMY [Parents to Adopt Minority Youngsters] in Minnesota, and the Children's Service Centre in Montreal ... we are finding out about the kind of people whose desire to be parents can be fulfilled in loving and rearing children who need them. These people regard racial differences as only one of the several differences to be acknowledged and dealt with in rearing an adopted child.[40]

Here, racial differences stand in for much more complex issues of citizenship status, racialization processes, capitalism, and imperialism. When we are not attentive to *how* children become adoptable—or attractive to adoptive parents—we cannot fully understand the complexities of these adoptions and their impacts both on the people involved and the larger culture.

All of these projects prioritized placing children of different racial groups and different citizenship statuses in white United States or Canadian adoptive homes. However, the highlighting of the IAP and ISS placement of Korean children in white U.S. families as keystones of this perspective on adoption is important. Both Korean adoptees and Native adoptees experience complications of both race *and* citizenship. It is also significant that the IAP and the placement of Korean children in American homes justified one another in more than multiple places in adoption archives. In both cases, these children had complicated citizenship status in the United States—for Native children of federally recognized tribes, dual citizenship, and for Korean children, non-citizenship in the United States until naturalization after their adoptions. In addition, both groups of children were often made adoptable because of the lack of material resources or support for child-rearing either in Indian Country or South Korea as a result of colonialism and war in both home territories.[41] CWLA's use of both projects as justification, and for allegedly illustrating the likelihood of success of the other, emphasizes how important both race and citizenship were in the adoption of these children into white U.S. adoptive homes.

The adoptions of Indigenous children and South Korean children into white homes in the United States have not continued at the same pace as in the twentieth century, largely due to governmental changes implemented after pressure from families and communities whose families had lost children to these processes. In the United States, that came in the form of ICWA, where federal law requires that Indigenous families and federally recognized communities have priority for any care of Indigenous children that occur outside of their family home. In the case of South Korea, these changes came in 2012, when the South Korean government changed the Special Adoption Act with the goal of having fewer children adopted by foreign families and retaining families. Despite both of these legal changes, both Korean and Indigenous children are still adopted into white American homes at higher levels than other populations. Some scholars have argued that both acts fail to address larger social structures that encourage the adoption of children or encourage parents—especially mothers and other birthing people—to not see themselves as able to raise their children.[42] We do not agree that these acts should not be enacted, but rather that they are not sufficient to address the impacts of transnational transracial adoption. Without question, these acts also fail to address the larger structures that encourage these adoptions in the first place—militarism, globalizing capitalism, and adoption as a form of family formation.

Notes

1 Kim Park Nelson, "Mapping multiple histories of Korean American transnational adoption," in *Contemporary Asian America (3rd Edition): A Multidisciplinary Reader*, eds. Ming Zhou and Anthony Christian Ocampo (2016) New York: New York University Press, 404–428, 408.
2 See Karen Balcomb, "Thinking with adoption in historical research," *Adoption & Culture* 6, no. 1 (2018): 15–17 and Kimberly D. McKee, *Disrupting Kinship: Transnational Politics of Korean Adoption in the United States*, Chicago: University of Illinois Press, 2019 for clarity around these histories.
3 "International adoption: Statistics," Holt International, http://www.holt international.org/insstats.shtml, as cited in Arissa H. Oh, *To Save the Children of Korea: The Cold War Origins of International Adoption*, Stanford: Stanford University Press, 2015: 2.
4 Barbara Melosh, *Strangers and Kin: The American Way of Adoption*, Cambridge: Harvard University Press, 2002: 105.
5 In this chapter and in the book more broadly, we use the terms Native and Indigenous interchangeably.
6 See essays in Lori Askeland, ed, *Children and Youth in Adoption, Orphanages, and Foster Care: A Historical Handbook and Guide*, Westport: Greenwood,

2006; Laura Briggs, *Taking Children: A History of American Terror*, Los Angeles: University of California Press, 2020; and Rickie Solinger, *Beggars and Choosers: How the Politics of Choice Shapes Adoption, Abortion, and Welfare in the United States*, New York: Hill and Wang, 2002. We also explore more about the best interests of the child legal doctrine in chapter 3 of this book.
7 For some examples, see McKee, *Disrupting Kinship*; Oh, *To Save the Children of Korea*; Kim Park Nelson, *Invisible Asians: Korean American Adoptees, Asian American Experiences, and Racial Exceptionalism*, New Brunswick: Rutgers University Press, 2016; SooJin Pate, *From Orphan to Adoptee: U.S. Empire and Genealogies of Korean Adoption*, Minneapolis: University of Minnesota Press, 2014; Susie Woo, *Framed by War: Korean Children and Women at the Crossroads of US Empire*, New York: NYU Press, 2019.
8 Park Nelson, "Mapping," 404.
9 Kelly Condit-Shrestha, "South Korea and adoption's ends: Reexamining the numbers and historicizing market economies," *Adoption & Culture*, 6, no. 2 (2018): 364–400, 365.
10 Report from Mrs. Alice Y. Moe to Mrs. Dorothy H. Sills, 9/14/1956: 1. Found in the Social Welfare History Archives at University of Minnesota, International Social Services—American Branch SW109.1, SW 109.1 (case records—access restricted), Case # Redacted."
11 Report from Mrs. Alice Y. Moe to Mrs. Dorothy H. Sills, 9/14/1956: 2. Found in the Social Welfare History Archives at University of Minnesota, International Social Services—American Branch SW109.1, SW 109.1 (case records—access restricted), Case # Redacted."
12 Many previously cited materials point to these connections. In addition, see Kristi Brian, *Reframing Transracial Adoption: Adopted Koreans, White Parents, and the Politics of Kinship*, Philadelphia: Temple University Press, 2012; Eleana J. Kim, *Adopted Territory: Transnational Korean Adoptees and the Politics of Belonging*, Durham: Duke University Press, 2010; and Hosu Kim, *Birth Mothers and Transnational Adoption Practice in South Korea: Virtual Mothering*, New York: Palgrave Macmillan, 2016.
13 Child Welfare League of America, "Our story," accessed August 8, 2023, at https://www.cwla.org/history/.
14 Joseph R. Reid, "Memo: American Indian Project," April 1, 1959. Found in the Social Welfare History Archives at University of Minnesota, Child Welfare League of America Records, Box 17 (Adoption), Folder 17/3, "Adoption-Indian Adoption Project: 1959–1962."
15 Ibid., n.p.
16 Child Welfare League of America, *Indian Adoption Project*, April, 1960. Found in the Social Welfare History Archives at University of Minnesota, Child Welfare League of America Records, Box 17 (Adoption), Folder 17/3, "Adoption-Indian Adoption Project: 1959–1962."
17 Ibid., 2.
18 Gwendolyn Mink, *Welfare's End*, Ithaca: Cornell University Press, 2001.
19 Child Welfare League of America, *The Indian Adoption Project—1958 through 1967: Report of Its Accomplishments, Evaluation, and Recommendations for Adoption Services to Indian Children*, April 1, 1968: 8. Found in the Social Welfare History Archives at University of Minnesota, Child Welfare League of America Records, Box 17 (Adoption), Folder 17/3, "Adoption-Indian Adoption Project: 1959–1962."
20 Zithra R. Turitz, "A new look at adoption: Current developments in the philosophy and practice of adoption," presented at CWLA Eastern Regional

Conference, 1965. Found in the Social Welfare History Archives at University of Minnesota, Folder 16/1, "Adoption—General, 1960–1965": 1.
21 Child Welfare League of America, *The Indian Adoption Project*: 7.
22 For more information on outing programs, see Kevin Whalen, *Native Students at Work: American Indian Labor and Sherman Institute's Outing Program, 1900–1945*, Seattle: University of Washington Press, 2016.
23 Child Welfare League of America Records. (1966, June 16). News Release, contact Isabel Johnson. Found in the Social Welfare History Archives at University of Minnesota, Folder 16:1, "Adoption: General, 1966–1969": 2.
24 Ibid., 3
25 David Fanshel, *Far from the reservation: The transracial adoption of American Indian Children*, Metuchen, N.J.: Scarecrow Press, 1972: 21.
26 Though most non-Indigenous Americans understand enrollment in federally recognized tribes as requiring a certain "percentage" of indigenous heritage, not all tribes require this. For example, the Cherokee Nation determines tribal enrollment according to documented connection to an enrolled lineal Cherokee Nation ancestor who is listed on the Dawes Roll, taken between 1899 and 1906 of citizens and freedpeople in Indian Territory, which is now northeast Oklahoma (Cherokee Nation Tribal Registration).
27 Kazuyo Kubo, "Desirable difference: The shadow of racial stereotypes in creating transracial families through transnational adoption," *Sociology Compass 4*, no. 4 (2010): 263–282, 281.
28 Barbara Katz Rothman, *Weaving a Family: Untangling Race and Adoption*, Boston: Beacon Press (2006): 107.
29 Sidney Talisman, "Report on Visit to Korea—June 24 to July 2, 1968, p. 11. Found in the social welfare history archives at University of Minnesota, International Social Services—American Branch SW109.1, Folder SW0109, "ISSAB Korea: Administrative Correspondence, 1968–1992."
30 Margaret A. Valk, "Korean-American children in American adoptive homes," presented at National Conference on Social Welfare, Philadelphia, PA, 11/1/1957, 1.
31 Wells C. Klein, "Letter to Mr. Sidney Talisman," 19 Feb 1971, n.p. found in the social welfare history archives at University of Minnesota, International Social Services—American Branch SW109.1, Folder SW0109, "ISSAB Korea-Adoptions (folder 1 of 5) 1976–1978."
32 Briggs, *Taking Children*, 49.
33 Kim TallBear, *Native American DNA: Tribal Belonging and the False Promise of Genetic Science*, Minneapolis: University of Minnesota Press, 2013: 45.
34 Joanne Barker, *"Indian-made": Sovereignty and the work of identification* (Doctoral Dissertation), 2001. Retrieved from ProQuest. (9979914).
35 Patricia Cotter-Busbee and Trace A. DeMeyer (eds.), *Two worlds: Lost children of the Indian Adoption Project*, Greenfield, MA: Blue Hand Books, 2013; and Trace A. DeMeyer, *One Small Sacrifice: Lost Children of the Indian Adoption Project*, Greenfield, MA: Blue Hand Books, 2012.
36 Fanshel, *Far from the reservation*, 25.
37 Ibid., 341.
38 Turitz, "A new Look at adoption": 5.
39 Ibid.
40 Ibid., 7.
41 McKee, *Disrupting Kinship*; D.S. Kim, "A country divided: Contextualizing adoption from a Korean perspective," in *International Korean adoption: A fifty-year history of policy and practice*, 3–23; Claire Palmiste, "From the Indian

Adoption Project to the Indian Child Welfare Act: the resistance of Native American communities," *Indigenous Policy Journal*, 22, no. 1 (2011): 1–10; Raven Sinclair, "Identity lost and found: Lessons from the sixties scoop," *First Peoples Child & Family Review*, 3, no. 1 (2007): 65–82.

42 Russell Lawrence Barsh, "Indian Child Welfare Act of 1978: A critical analysis," *The Hastings Law Journal 31* (1979): 1287–1336; Manuel P. Guerrero, "Indian Child Welfare Act of 1978: A response to the threat to Indian culture caused by foster and adoptive placements of Indian children," *American Indian Law Review*, 7, no. 1 (1979): 51–77; Sook K. Kim, "Abandoned babies: The backlash of South Korea's Special Adoption Act," *Washington International Law Journal* 24, no. 3 (2015): 709–726; Marc Mannes, "Factors and events leading to the passage of the Indian Child Welfare Act," *Center for Social Research and Development*, 25 (1995): 350–357.

CONSTELLATIONS OF NATIONAL ECONOMIES, FAMILY SEPARATION, AND MILITARY OCCUPATION IN THE TRANSNATIONAL ADOPTION INDUSTRIAL COMPLEX

Interlude with Kimberly D. McKee

Kimberly D. McKee is an associate professor in the School of Interdisciplinary Studies at Grand Valley State University. She is the author of *Disrupting Kinship: Transnational Politics of Korean Adoption in the United States* (University of Illinois Press, 2019) and *Adoption Fantasies: The Fetishization of Asian Adoptees from Girlhood to Womanhood* (The Ohio State University Press, 2023), as well as the co-editor of *Degrees of Difference: Reflections of Women of Color on Graduate School* (University of Illinois Press, 2020). McKee serves as a co-chair of the executive committee for the Alliance of the Study of Adoption and Culture.

Tanya Bakhru: What brought you to the work that you're doing?
Kimberly McKee: I arrived at my work in Adoption Studies when I was completing my Master's Degree. I hold a master's degree in Gender and Social Policy from the London School of Economics. When I was doing that work, I was thinking about what my Master's thesis would focus on. It was either going to look at the gendered reasons why South Korea still participates in international adoption, or it was going to look at military camp towns and Korean sex workers. Regardless, it was all going to be related to adoption. I opted to focus on the former, and that stems from my own positionality. I'm a transnational Korean adoptee. I was adopted into the United States and raised by white parents. My own interest in thinking through the systemic reasons fueling international adoption is

DOI: 10.4324/9781003303442-6

	how I arrived at this work. For those unfamiliar, South Korea has been participating in international adoption since the post-Korean War period. We're talking decades-long engagement, even as the nation became one of the largest world economies. A recent documentary highlighting the rise of international adoption alongside economic development is Deann Borshay Liem's *Geographies of Kinship* (2019), which tracks the experiences of Korean international adoptees.
Bakhru:	How has your research changed over the years, and what are the different issues that emerged that are unexpected or particularly interesting?
McKee:	When thinking about my research trajectory, a lot has changed since I completed my Master's Degree more than fifteen years ago. I took a break between my master's and my PhD. When I returned to get my PhD, I still decided to pursue an interest in Korean international adoption, but I was really invested in listening to and centering the voices of adult adoptees. Too often in adoption studies or even in conversations around adoption—informally or in popular media—adoptees are always rendered as perpetual children. We never really see adoptees as adults, let alone experts on adoption. And here, I'm not thinking about experts like a social welfare practitioner. Rather, I am thinking about experts as the people who've actually lived adoption. What does it mean to listen to adoptees? It means to recognize that there are adoptees who are parents, who are grandparents, who are also trained and work in the field. We need to recognize that their expertise is just as valid as some adoptive parents who are also in the field of adoption studies. Often, those folks are seen as impartial in ways that adoptees aren't when we talk about members from marginalized communities engaging in research on those very same communities, right? When I initially started thinking about this as a graduate student and when I completed my first book, *Disrupting Kinship: Transnational Politics of Korean Adoption in the United States* (University of Illinois Press, 2019), I was intentional about wanting to highlight the history of Korean adoption, but not necessarily focus on it. There are some lovely books by some fabulous scholars documenting those histories—for example, the work of

Tobias Hübinette, Susie Woo, Kori Graves, SooJin Pate, or Arissa Oh. Eleana J. Kim and Kim Park Nelson also do that work while foregrounding the adopted Korean community. I was invested in exploring what these histories look like in relation to what I call "the transnational adoption industrial complex"—the neo-colonial, multi-million-dollar industry that commodifies children's bodies. This was in addition to grappling with broader questions of citizenship and family, locating adult adoptees as experts of their own experiences, and engaging adoptee activism. That's what my first book focuses on. In my subsequent work, I continue to locate adoptees as experts. This includes listening to and amplifying adoptee voices in documentaries and literature, examining adoptee participation in a national organization aimed at supporting Korean adoptees and adoptive families, and situating some of my own experiences in some of this work. Some of my more recent publications include my own personal reflections in a way that I did not feel comfortable doing in my first book because I didn't want my identity as an adoptee to somehow subvert the legibility or the credibility within the academy of my actual expertise on adoption.

My more recent book, *Adoption Fantasies: The Fetishization of Asian Adoptees from Girlhood to Womanhood* (Ohio State University Press, 2023), considers the reverberations and effects of sensationalist and fictional adoption portrayals in the lives of adopted women and girls. This book interrogates the limits and contours of multiculturalism and colorblindness in analyzing racialized and sexualized popular culture representations of Asian adopted women and girls from 1992 to 2015. As I wrote my conclusion, I realized this is my love letter to other Asian adopted women and girls. I am creating the book that I wish I had access to and that other adoptees had access to when we were growing up because the work that I do is not solely meant for academics. I want my writings to be accessible to adoptees, as well as adoptive parents, adoption agency officials, etc. *Adoption Fantasies* is the project where I'm trying to locate our experiences as Asian adoptees. What does it mean when your white adoptive parents were not prepared to and didn't want to reckon with the ways your body was going to undergo sexualization and racialization? How many adoptive parents are complicit in that when thinking about how they talk about infant girl bodies as being cute? Or when thinking about scholars, such as Sara Dorow or Heather Jacobson, who write about adoptive parents that they've interviewed who refer to their Chinese-adopted daughters as "China dolls." What does that actually look like and feel like, and how does that get manifested in these other kinds of contexts?

Krista Benson: Earlier, when you mentioned how your work has evolved, you used a term that you use throughout your work, "the transnational adoption industrial complex." Could you tell us a little bit about that idea? How is it useful to see transnational adoption through that lens?

McKee: The transnational adoption industrial complex, as I conceived of it, engages the multiple assemblages that allow international adoption to be possible to operate together—sometimes synchronously, but a lot of times asynchronously. I'm invested in understanding the ways orphanages in "sending" countries and adoption agencies in "receiving" countries work to facilitate transnational adoption. This requires attention to legislation in both countries. Here, I am thinking about the laws that rendered children adoptable, as well as the laws that facilitated adoptees' entry into the United States, for example, because Asian adoptees were simultaneously circumventing racist exclusionary immigration laws. I'm also interested in, and this is something that I don't talk about in my publications, how other industries benefited from international adoption, such as the airline industry. No one really talks about airlines and their relation to adoption unless they're talking about Operation Babylift, and yet those airlines were making money from the transfer of children. I also consider the ways children were rendered adoptable as orphans or as adoptees as they move from being orphans to being adoptable. SooJin Pate and Susie Woo write about that in their work. It's important to know that Mirah Riben has a book where she's talking about the adoption industrial complex in relation to domestic adoption, and that book is called *The Stork Market: America's Multibillion Dollar Unregulated Adoption*

Industry (2006). That book does not necessarily get highlighted enough when we're talking about a lot of this work. What I'm really invested in is thinking about how South Korea laid the groundwork for other international adoption streams. I argue that China learned from Korea when they hosted the 2008 Beijing Olympics. To understand how different laws were being put in place around adoption prior to the Beijing Olympics, you really need to look at the Seoul Games in 1988. Korea was chastised by the West for adoptees being one of their largest exports. I find the reaction by Western countries to be completely ironic because the West was and is the largest consumer of international adoptees, specifically the United States. And so, when we think about these sorts of lessons learned, or when we think about what happens when you see how interconnected some of these pieces that seem so disconnected are, Korea demonstrates again how to create a functional adoption economy, and that makes people uncomfortable. People don't like thinking about international adoption as a form of buying and selling children, except that it is, right? This is why you hear a lot of gift language being used. People don't like feeling that or finding out that a country's adoption fees really reflect racist beliefs about Black and brown people. And yet, that's where we are.

Benson: Do you want to say anything about the economy of the reunion industry in the context of international adoption?

McKee: I'm more than happy to talk about the economy of the reunion industry because I gestured toward that in terms of thinking about the airline industry when we talk about the reunions or even the market of returning. Consider all those different motherland tours, or heritage tours or homeland tours, or whatever you want to call it, that bring international adoptees to their countries of origin. We're seeing the way in which culture becomes commodified in different kinds of ways, right? No longer is it that the commodification of culture is happening at heritage camps in North America and elsewhere. Rather, it's about the temple visits, the food making, the ways in which adoptees are creating kinship with one another or their families.

It's also about the dollars being injected into those economies. For example, I am referring to buying a ticket on Korean Air, the hotel stays, and the amount of money being injected into the economy through food, through buying gifts or cultural tchotchkes, or beauty products or stocks or glasses. It is also important to think about reunions with your Korean family and what that looks like in terms of other kinds of monetization happening through those reunions. This is not to say all reunions involve an exchange of either money or gifts, but once you arrive somewhere, it's very hard to not spend any money just by the virtue of being a human who needs to survive. You are at least spending something on lodging and even basic food. So, even if you're not going out and having an extravagant meal, you're still injecting money into the local economy. We need to think about what that looks like in the context of the transnational adoption industrial complex.

What's interesting, though is the fact that, for the most part, now there's an infrastructure facilitating returns. When Korean adoptees started returning in the late 1980s and '90s, folks weren't ready. People assume that adoptees were taking a one-way trip, and yet the transnational adoption industrial complex has adjusted itself to then fulfill these new needs. This also includes when adoptees are going back to their orphanages and requesting access to their adoption files. Scholars like Kim Park Nelson and Eleana J. Kim demonstrate that recordkeeping, and what adoptees have access to, is always in flux and ever-changing. Adoptees talk about this informally amongst themselves, but Park Nelson and Kim lend scholarly credence to that in terms of their own findings and their ethnographic oral history work.

Bakhru: I really appreciate the idea of the transnational adoption industrial complex because these processes are transnational and global, and they intersect with each other, and they create situations where, as individuals and communities, they may be separated by thousands of miles, what they are experiencing is similar, right? Part of globalization is creating a market out of things that were previously not part of the market. In the 1980s and '90s, the experiences you are talking about became commodified, and they will continue to become commodified because that's how neo-colonialism and global capitalism works. Their tentacles reach out and start bringing things into the marketplace that previously were not, and a lot of what you are talking about reminds me of other industries like ecotourism or any other kind of tourism, which then becomes an economic development strategy and becomes explicitly written into the ways that countries formulate themselves and develop their economies.

McKee: What you are saying really acknowledges the way how the TAIC maps onto all these other nations. You're already seeing it a little bit in terms of China. It's going to increase as Chinese adoptees enter adulthood and have their own income to make these decisions outside of their adoptive parents. You're going to see it more and more as they stake their own claims. You're seeing this too in the shifts of who is studying Chinese international adoption and who contributes to scholarly conversations around Korean international adoption.

Bakhru: At its core, the reproductive justice framework centers a human rights approach. How does a human rights framework apply to the work that you do?

McKee: First, I believe that adoption is a Reproductive Justice issue. That has to be clearly acknowledged and stated. It is important to think about how does the right to parent intersects with adoption. We're seeing this in terms of the right to parent a child, as well as a child's right to access to their origins. It's continually being questioned, and it's fraught. Not only is it fraught because of the way in which the current political climate is making it fundamentally clear that there is a certain contingent who's trying to force women to carry children, and that forced pregnancy is related to the creation of available white babies for adoption. We're also seeing restrictions overall, in terms of access to making family planning decisions. Within my own work, I consider: What does it mean to utilize that [Reproductive Justice] framework, which was first rooted within Black feminism? What does that look like when we consider other cultural contexts? What does that look like if we're talking about [Reproductive Justice] in terms of birth mothers' rights in South Korea or when we talk about unwed mothers' activism in Korea to raise awareness? What does that look like in terms of adoptee activism in South Korea to support those unwed mothers? And what in terms of working in coalition? How do we understand international adoption when adoptive parents, the largest consumers of children, are bemoaning different pieces of legislation that are designed to support family preservation because it slows down their adoptions or feels unnecessary?

It is important to think about reproductive justice as a human rights approach in times of political and military crises. For example, what is happening with Ukrainian children in Eastern Europe in the context of the war in Ukraine, or what emerged as the U.S. withdrew from Afghanistan? Or what happened with Haiti after the 2008 earthquake, as well as Operation Babylift? It is really important to think about whose human rights we are centering and whose humanity is legible in these conversations. When we then go back to this question about Reproductive Justice and how I firmly believe adoption is a Reproductive Justice issue, it is critical to examine the conditions that compel people to relinquish their children.

Another way to think about this is: What does it mean to create a policy that does not support economically precarious families? Because for the most part, when you're talking about children relinquished in South Korea, it went from postwar economic precarity to a lack of social welfare safety net to support single-mother households and economically precarious families during decades of rapid industrialization and urbanization in the 1960s to 1980s.

We also see this in the United States in relation to foster care and the way in which the foster care system is punitively designed as an arm of the carceral state to render children separate. Overall, it's about asking what it means when folks are decrying the dearth of available children for adoption. The panic is usually in relation to the dearth of available white children or international adoptees, who are not seen as children of color by their adoptive parents. There is never a panic about the Black and brown children in foster care. And if there is, it's because Black and brown children are fetishized in harmful ways that deny their full humanity. If we were really in the business of caring for kids, we would be focused on family preservation. We would be focused on supporting and creating systems where children who need to be in care for a variety of reasons are in environments that are actually nurturing and facilitate connections with community members in deeper ways that are meaningful, as opposed to trying to undermine legislation like ICWA, for example.

To add on to that, we see this in the *Dobbs* v. *Jackson Women's Health Organization* (2022) U.S. Supreme Court decision and the way adoption is weaponized as an alternative to abortion. It's not an alternative (see *Adoption & Culture* 2023 special issue on the subject). I was also grappling with these questions for my essay that is part of the Adoption, Family Separation & Preservation, and Reproductive Justice digital symposia organized by Gretchen Sisson.[1]

Moreover, in conversations about adoption, family separation, preservation, and Reproductive Justice, birth mother voices are still less visible. We need to figure out more generally, as we're having conversations both about foster care and adoption, how are we doing it in a way that is inclusive to ensure we're not speaking for them while recognizing the vulnerability of speaking out and honoring that as well.

Benson: Is there anything else you want to share with us about the relationship you see between Reproductive Justice frameworks and adoption and foster care systems, specifically within the U.S., positioning the U.S. as a "receiving company" country in the framing of transnational adoption?

McKee: When talking about Reproductive Justice in the lens of international adoption, it's not just thinking about adoptees whose parents intentionally sought international adoption. We also need to talk about those children forcibly separated from their parents at the U.S.-Mexico border, as well as those children who were born in the United States whose immigrant parents have been deported back to their countries of origin. These conversations should not be happening separately. We also need to think about forced separation as a form of international adoption in terms of children being laundered through the U.S. foster care system. We need to have a deeper conversation about what's happening with the Indian Child Welfare Act and the long-term implications of *Brackeen* v. *Haaland* (2023). We cannot think of these issues in an individualized or siloed way. Another issue to consider is how parents or guardians failed to naturalize their international adoptees as U.S. citizens. That's a huge policy failure. When we think about calls for retroactive citizenship for those adoptees, we also have to ask ourselves: What are we doing for other undocumented people? What are we doing about children who were brought to the United States as children, so they didn't really have any kind of agency over those decisions, as well as their parents? How are they different? Why are undocumented individuals who were brought to the United States being treated so differently than international adoptees whose parents failed to act on their citizenship? I think we know why. I think we recognize the way white supremacy operates, right? For me, all of these things are interconnected.

When folks talk about adoption, it's really important to include foster care. Here, I'm specifically thinking about adoption not only as a method of care but also as an analytic [tool] to help understand white supremacy, settler colonialism, militarism, and imperialism and how the transitional adoption industrial complex maps onto these broader concepts. What does it mean when we recognize the damaging effects of Christian Americanism — a term Arissa Oh has coined — alongside white supremacy in relation to adoption in state care? How can we recognize the legacy of adoptee activism as part of these conversations? Often, I think about the intellectual genealogy of these issues. This is not only about the scholars who came before, who created the field of Critical Adoption Studies, as well as Adoption Studies broadly. This includes the adoptee activism that was occurring prior to the rise of Twitter, TikTok, and [other] forms of social media. It's about acknowledging the ways birth parents were organizing prior to social media and connecting with one another, and about the adult adoptee organizations emerging in the 1980s and the 1990s and then really exploding right around the turn of the twenty-first century because of Web 2.0 platforms building on the

	use of listservs and blogs. Broadly speaking, when we're talking about any form of activism, it just didn't happen overnight. Having those conversations is really hard in a space like Twitter because Twitter does not allow for the kinds of nuance that we need to have to grapple with these issues. Twitter sometimes only allows for the loudest voice in the room to be heard. While I think Twitter communities are valuable, and I'm on Twitter, I also think we need to be recognizing how Twitter fits in with these longer trajectories of adoptees' networking, of activism happening, and of people shifting the needle.
Bakhru:	It is really important to bring these different ideas into conversation with each other because we can't be focusing on one thing without focusing on the other. I really appreciate you saying that adoption is an analytic [tool] to look at these different systems. That is helping me to think about these larger transnational issues in a different way.
Benson:	Absolutely.
McKee:	It's important because we have to look at who's helping facilitate resettlement, who is helping facilitate the foster care placement of children separated from the border, what that looked like, and how faith-based adoption agencies, in particular, are revenue streams. At the end of the day, it's about money. You need to follow the money because that's what people are interested in. Again, if people were truly interested about the well-being of children, the whole system would look fundamentally different.
Benson:	Rhetorically, when we talk about popular conceptions of adoption, it is all about children's well-being, which covers up a lot of pretty ugly stuff around how adoption actually functions. I will never forget, reading toward the end of your book, when you actually were comparing the country fees for adoption from different countries, and how blatantly apparent that was set up to show the various valuations of racial difference and how neatly those aligned with different kinds of fees from different for international adoptions in different countries. It was really disturbing.
McKee:	I did find that the fee from Haiti if I remember, increased following the earthquake. This is how markets operate and what that looks like. You cannot engage with this work with the faint of heart because we're talking about the separation of children from their parents and because

of the overall discomfort produced when you realize that we're talking about actual people. You have some level of detachment or at least dark humor as you're having these conversations because it is demoralizing, right? It's demoralizing when you realize that some of the earliest adoption creative fiction comes from those folks who wrote orphan social studies. Those are the people who describe adopted children to their adoptive parents. What I found in my research with my first book was that a lot of those descriptions were very similar. What does that mean when these seemingly unique details are not seemingly unique; they're very much from a template? That is hard for folks to want to grapple with, right? People don't want to see the ways adoption is a system and institution. Sometimes, I think people don't necessarily recognize how theoretically complex adoption is because that means challenging internalized beliefs about what an adoption is supposed to be.

Benson: Absolutely. There can be a defensiveness that a lot of people will get even if they themselves are not adoptive parents. Like, why are you saying my brother is a bad person? But actually, we are talking about a much more complicated thing than that statement.

McKee: Yes. So, I'm really clear that I am talking about systems and institutions. I am not talking about individual people. I've had my fair share of those kinds of conversations, and it's important to note that some of those conversations are happening with other scholars. Feminists need to reckon with the complexities of adoption. If they aren't reckoning with those complexities now, they sure as hell need to be reckoning with them, as access to various forms of reproductive health care are being undermined. To build effective coalitions, we need to recognize the way adoption is a feminist issue, and not in the way like, "Oh, we need to adopt the babies," but in a "We need to support family preservation" [way]. And we need to support women's and pregnant people's autonomy over their bodies. We need to consider what it means to be both an adoptive parent and a feminist. How do you leverage your privilege in a variety of ways to support bodily autonomy and family preservation for the marginalized without getting in your feelings about it?

	The latter part is the most important because it's actually not about people as individuals.

Even as folks are reading this, I'm sure there might be folks pearl-clutching, but if you truly want to put your money where your mouth is in terms of your feminist values, then what are you actually doing about it? How are you amplifying the voices of folks critiquing the systems? I don't think adoption will necessarily go away, but we need to transform it. This is not to say that I don't agree with folks working toward the abolition of foster care or adoption. Rather, for us to even move that needle to get to that point, there will be micro-steps that need to happen in between. |
| *Bakhru:* | That really gets to the heart of the matter, which is: How do we conceptualize care? How do we conceptualize the value of differently embodied, gendered, racialized people? And as you said: How do some people's humanity become legible and other people's don't? |
| *McKee:* | Yeah, what does it say when you accept the children of the people you don't want in your country? What does that actually mean? And what does it tell your child? Because children are listening, and adult adoptees of color can talk to you about the racism they've experienced in their own families and from their adoptive parents. What's important when thinking about abolition is—I'm in agreement—What does that actually look like? I can't speak to foster care because that's not my area of expertise, but to fully abolish transnational adoption also involves working with a variety of state governments and other countries. If we're going to have these conversations, we have to think about how systemically embedded adoption has [prevented] the creation of social welfare policies to support families. And so, if we're going to talk about abolition in the case of adoption, what is the context? Because that context matters. |

Note

1 https://blog.petrieflom.law.harvard.edu/symposia/adoption/

4
JUVENILE JUSTICE, FOSTER CARE, AND ADOPTION

On April 20, 2021, 16-year-old Ma'khia Bryant was shot four times by a police officer and died.[1] She was killed outside of the foster home that she'd been living in for less than three months. She was living in foster care in the home where multiple 911 calls had been placed in the last several years, including one made just a couple of months before. That call was placed by Ma'Khia's younger sister, also placed in this foster home, who was threatening to kill someone in the home if she wasn't placed in another home. The children were not removed from the home after that call.[2]

Bryant and her siblings had been removed from their mother's custody three years prior after the children alleged that their mother had physically abused them, which she denies. For the first sixteen months, the children lived with their grandmother, Jeanene Hammonds, but they were removed due to a conflict between their grandmother and mother in 2019. When Hammonds petitioned to have the children placed back in her care in December 2019, Franklin County Children's Services (FCCS) denied the placement, citing her previous failure to get the children in therapy. From that point on, the Bryant children were placed in non-family foster homes, in contrast to one of FCCS' stated guiding principles: "We recognize that children are best served within their family and community."[3] From December 2019 to April 2021, both girls were placed in non-family foster homes.

Ma'khia Bryant came into contact with police the day that they killed her because of her placement in the juvenile justice system. The police were called on April 20 due to an argument between Ma'khia and two former residents of the foster home.[4] After the police bodycam video of her killing went viral, a group mostly comprised of other young Black girls and women

DOI: 10.4324/9781003303442-7

counteracted the sharing of her death by circulating the videos that Ma'khia made herself on her TikTok. As scholar Wendyliz Martinez writes, "the circulation of Bryant's TikToks ... showed her as a 'regular' young girl who liked to have fun online. We resisted the narrative of her being a 'dangerous' youth, a person that deserved their fate. She is preserved in a moment of time where she is happy."[5] The labor of activists, scholars, and social media users like Martinez highlight the importance of resisting the media's way of framing Ma'Khia Bryant and other youth like her, focusing on who they were when they were alive, not only the circumstances of their deaths.

In 2010, 254,375 children entered foster care in the United States, and it is estimated that 408,425 children are in foster placements at any given point.[6] Hundreds of thousands of children and their families are affected by this system every year, and not all of the impacts are good ones. One impact that should be more widely known is that children in the foster care system are at increased risk of being involved in the juvenile justice system on criminal charges or status offenses. For those children who are involved in both systems, most of them started in the foster care system and then entered into the juvenile justice system.[7] While many Americans are, to some degree, now aware of the school-to-prison pipeline, fewer people are aware of the foster care-to-juvenile justice pipeline.

In this chapter, we explore the porous boundaries between the juvenile justice system and the systems of child welfare and family policing in the United States. Though we include the foster care system, we do not limit this analysis to children in formal state foster care. This is because

> [c]hildren who have been placed in state custody or under state supervision are also placed in family homes (their homes of origin, relatives or other kinship care), sometimes with a formal foster care designation if in kinship care but often not. Children and youth in state custody also are placed in group homes, mental hospitals, and juvenile correctional facilities. By focusing only on children in foster care, a limited and perhaps skewed view is developed.[8]

In many states, the juvenile courts also handle cases of children who have not been accused of criminal activity but are being neglected, abused, or those who are "beyond the control of their parents."[9] As we show in this chapter, the intertwining of family policing systems, foster care, and the juvenile justice system is vital to understand when we consider the use of the foster care system, specifically, as an issue of Reproductive Justice.

Dorothy Roberts defines the child welfare system or, in her words, the family policing system, as "the assemblage of public and private child protection agencies, foster care, and preventive services," and, as she notes, this system "is a crucial part of the carceral machinery in Black communities."[10] Indeed, Black social workers, scholars, and activists were some of the first to draw attention to the ways that foster care and family policing are more broadly used as a form of U.S. government-sponsored family restructuring that particularly targeted Black families. In 1972, Andrew Billingsley and Jeanne M. Giovanni's *Children of the Storm: Black Children and American Child Welfare* brought national attention to the overrepresentation of Black children in American foster care systems in 1972, highlighting this overrepresentation was a product of both changed child welfare processes and changed migration patterns of Black families.[11] In the same year, the National Council for Black Social Workers issued a position statement on transracial adoptions and foster care where they stated that they had taken "a vehement stand against the placement of Black children in white homes for any reason. We affirm the inviolable position of Black children in Black families where they belong physically, psychologically, and culturally."[12] These social workers and academics made strong cases for the importance of Black children being raised by Black families. And yet Black children—and Indigenous children—are still disproportionately raised in foster care in the United States.

Indigenous and women of color feminists have long-advanced insights about state repression and rejection of anti-radical and neoliberal strategies for justice.[13] These theorists reject the promises of liberalism—such as the usefulness of state-recognized rights or protections—and deny that the liberal state is the place to look for solutions to violence. Instead, they argue, it is vital to be critical of the ways that state violence can be hidden when examining the status of Indigenous people and people of color. Historically, in the United States, the enmeshment of state power and family policing have guaranteed that "certain cultural forms of mothering [and parenting] have been privileged while, while others have been penalized."[14] The removal of Black and Indigenous children from their families of origin is a part of the family policing system in the U.S. design, not an accidental result of the system.

Juvenile justice and foster care are both systems that are managed and regulated at the state and county level. This means that there are anywhere between fifty and more than one thousand different iterations of these systems, their rules, and the guidelines for how youth should or can be treated. This complex web of systems means that the youth who are most likely to be under state family surveillance and thus put into these systems are also more likely to be separated from their families. This chapter demonstrates that when Reproductive Justice theory and practice are applied to these systems, the most compelling option is the abolition of our current juvenile justice and foster care systems. We argue that they should be supplanted with supportive programs for families, reallocation of resources to impoverished communities, and community-run and community-accountable processes to ensure the well-being of children in our communities.

"Child Savers": The Establishment of Juvenile Justice and Family Court Systems in the United States

Though both the juvenile justice system and family court system seem normalized to many USians, the development of these systems is relatively new. A separate civil procedure for addressing criminal behavior, abuse, and neglect of children has not always been in place in the United States. Until the 1800s, children were tried, convicted, and sentenced as adults in adult courts, and neglected or abused children were held in adult prisons.

At the turn of the twentieth century, social reformers attempted to change child welfare policies, which we refer to as family policing policies. These crusaders conceived of child welfare reform as a wide-ranging social reform movement to address children's problems, creating juvenile courts, opposing child labor, implementing mandatory school attendance laws for all students, and founding charitable and then governmental departments dedicated to child safety and welfare.[15] This reform resulted in the establishment of what would become family courts, which manage child custody, the foster care system, and the juvenile justice system.

The child welfare reformers who lobbied for these statutes originally conceived of the challenges of children in need as connected to social problems, such as poverty. These reformers "approached juvenile misbehavior not as a crime, but rather as a disease that could be diagnosed and cured. This philosophy was soon expanded to include the belief that maladjusted behavior could also be prevented by active intervention in the early stages of the child's development."[16] Though arguably an improvement over incarcerating all children in adult jails, this system still treated child delinquency as a social disease and delinquent children as symptoms of that disease. This philosophy led to the establishment of civil, juvenile justice systems. The first juvenile court in the nation was established in 1899 in Cook County, Illinois. Other states quickly followed this example.[17] Juvenile justice systems, their policies, and procedures differ greatly from state to state and even county to county. With this understanding, the needs of children must be addressed at a social level, including work reform projects, to increase poor people's standard of living.

Because the child savers saw the previous punishment of children in adult courts as unnecessarily harsh, they established the "best interests of the child" under the legal doctrine *parens patriae*. This legal doctrine originated in medieval English courts and allowed the monarch to intervene in family matters, which supported the stability of the state. In the United States, this doctrine was first used to justify a civil court's intervention in placing a girl at a "house of refuge," despite her father's resistance, in 1838.[18] This doctrine was embraced by the creators of the juvenile court, as it "provided a rather murky justification for state intervention into the lives of children. Because the state considered that it had a profound interest in seeing that its children grew up to be moral, virtual, and productive members of society, it utilized the *parens patriae* doctrine to fulfill this goal."[19]

Under this doctrine, the juvenile courts established that juvenile sentencing should be individualized and all decisions should be made in the "best interest of the child." In theory, this should allow for a fairer, more just system. In reality, it puts a tremendous amount of control in the hands of judges, prosecutors, and juvenile defense attorneys. Unsurprisingly, many legal scholars have critiqued this doctrine as detrimental to youth of color, Indigenous youth, youth in the foster care system, and LGBTQ+ youth.[20] In short, the best interest of the child is being determined by a juvenile justice system that moves within and supports a racist, heterosexist, cissexist, and settler state. The best interests of the child doctrine, the ways that juvenile courts were established, and the vast reach of authority of the juvenile courts over vulnerable youth's lives emphasize the power of the juvenile court in justice-involved youth's lives.

Though the family policing system began with language and practice that at least gestured toward justice and family stability, beginning in the late 1950s and into the 1970s, social welfare practitioners moved toward an increasingly punitive stance on what they saw as child welfare. This changed stance led to the increasing use of child removal for abuse or neglect in the foster care system and the increasing use of the juvenile justice system as a punitive force.[21] These professional moves toward child removal impacted both family courts considering the best interest of the child in home placement and in the increasing use of the juvenile justice system for behaviors that did not violate the law or which only violated the law when the person is a minor.

Status offenses are the category of behavior that are illegal only because a person is a minor. These include things like truancy, breaking curfew, running away from home, and other actions that are legal for adults to take but not children. In 2020, an estimated 57,700 status offenses were handled in juvenile courts, which is a much smaller number of cases from earlier in the 2000s. This is partially attributed to the beginning of the COVID-19 pandemic in 2020, the closures of schools—which often refer students to the juvenile justice system—and changing federal policies that encourage the reduced use of status offenses for youth.[22] Even with the closure of many schools and moves to online learning, 58% of these cases were referred for truancy.

Contemporary Child-Saving

Juvenile carceral research is now increasingly focused on the role that race, class, and gender have in the criminalization and punishment of youth in the United States. One important finding is that both young boys and girls of color and Indigenous people in impoverished communities have been disproportionately marked as violent, and there is an increase in the criminalization of previously non-criminal behavior and the up-charging of status offenses.[23] Rios explores the impact of pervasive criminalization of Black and Latino boys' behavior, which has led to these youth being trapped in a punitive system that consistently uses race, socioeconomic status, and the negative views of society to subject adolescent boys to circular systems of stigmatization. As a result of this ongoing policing, these boys tend to internalize their assigned criminality and attempt to defy the system by taking on the delinquent roles society expects them to uphold.[24]

Similarly, scholars looking at the rhetoric of the drastic increase in girls' violence since the 1990s find that, though this rhetoric has been increasingly used by scholars and the media and that girls' rates of confinement are increasing, there is no quantitative proof that girls are actually more violent.[25] Males also point to the ways in which pathologizing and criminalizing girls as a group has stood in the place of analysis that considers the real relationship between girls' incarceration and the poverty, abuse, and racial disadvantages they experience.[26] These studies show that it is not that girls are getting more violent but that they're more likely to be arrested and incarcerated for offenses such as arguments with their parents or fighting in schools, which would have been classified as a status offense or ignored prior to the rise of "zero-tolerance" policies, wherein youth who are accused of violence in schools are automatically referred to the juvenile justice system for delinquency charges.[27] "This pattern suggests that the social control of girls is once again on the criminal justice agenda, with a crucial change. In this century, the control is being justified by girls' 'violence,' which is a new way of framing older and previously non-criminal behaviors."[28] This same pattern emerges for boys, wherein zero-tolerance policies combined with what Rios terms "the youth control complex"—the criminalization of non-illegal behaviors such as truancy or "talking back" to teachers—can lead to engagement with the juvenile justice system and codes these behaviors as violent and criminal.[29]

These authors also discuss the ways in which race and gender expectations placed specifically on youth of color in impoverished areas impact their relationships with authority figures and the ways that their survival strategies are interpreted. Rios found that probation and police officers expect the Black and Latino boys and young men to exhibit their masculinity by standing up to their delinquent friends and abiding by the law. However, due to a lack of resources to follow this plan effectively, the marginalized youth are forced to exhibit the hypermasculinity of the street through toughness, aggressiveness, and resistance.[30] For these youth, "the gender ideals purveyed by police, probation officers, and others did not translate adequately into the realities of the boys' lives."[31] Because they are positioned as young boys of color, the forms of masculinity expected by police and probation officers are heavily policed and, therefore, deeply tied to the likelihood of these youth being marked as criminals.

In a related study, Nikki Jones looks at the impacts of concerns with survival that are uniquely positioned in the framing and explaining of inner-city Black girls' violence and likely to mark them as violent and, therefore, criminal. These young women must both simultaneously set themselves up to survive in a violent environment while recognizing that "the need to avoid or overcome dangers throughout their adolescence presents a uniquely gendered challenge for girls who grow up in these neighborhoods."[32]

Thus, young Black women in inner cities feel that they must engage in particular forms of violence to survive the circumstances of their environment. Then, their violence becomes always-already, the presence that is always there, even if it's not currently being enacted. This always-already violence of Black girls explains why Black girls are read as more aggressive and more criminal than white girls, even if the acts they are committing are not themselves criminal acts.[33]

These ongoing forms of behavioral policing and gendered and racialized expectations have long-term impacts on youth, especially poor youth of color. For the young men in Rios' study, criminalization permanently impacted these youth's choices and led to circumstances where "crime and violence [were] some of the few resources for feeling dignity and empowerment."[34] Indeed, the state produces these options through the reorganization of the state's attention to the poor, where it is now prioritizing punitive institutions such as the police. This punitive structure, however, is not limited to formal punitive or welfare institutions. Chesney-Lind and Jones recognize that media and popular discourse also play into racial and gendered understandings of violence and criminality. Their book is set up to encourage readers to question media and political representations of girls as increasingly violent, offering empirical evidence that the moral panic resulting from this representation of girls is very harmful to the girls themselves, especially to girls of color who are more likely to live in highly policed urban areas. Informed by perspectives of feminist scholarship, these viewpoints emphasize the importance of understanding how gender, class, and race intersect to affect certain individuals unequally and how important it is for the voices of girls, especially disadvantaged girls, to be heard.

Reading these perspectives together, we see that there are strong race, gender, and class considerations in how youth are framed as criminal, and their behavior is marked as criminal, even when no violation of the law has occurred. For both boys and girls of color, in related but not identical ways, these gendered expectations, read through a racial and class lens, produce a legal and public fantasy in which their criminality and violence are assumed and, therefore, their eventual entry into juvenile detention is inevitable.

The juvenile justice system and the foster care systems' overlaps during their establishment at the turn of the twentieth century provide a clear indication of the ways that these systems *remain* intertwined. These relationships are woven through the structural setup of many foster care systems, including the use of juvenile court judges for at-risk child petitions for children in foster care and those in the care of their natal families.

In Washington State, for example, Senate Bill 5439 (1995), colloquially known as the Becca Bill, extended the powers of the juvenile court. The Becca Bill was named after a white teenage girl named Becca Hedman, who was murdered in Spokane in 1993 after a series of runaway attempts from her adoptive parents' home, group homes, and chemical dependency treatment centers after a childhood that contained two sexual assaults. Much of the media framing of Hedman's death and the activism of her family to encourage the use of status offenses to detain at-risk youth was tied to her whiteness and the need to protect (some) white girls from themselves.[35] The Becca Bill, posthumously named for Hedman, took the figure of the "running wild" white girl to justify the use of status offenses to detain youth at rates far beyond those of other states.

The bill provides strict enforcement of truancy laws; processes for involuntary confinement of youth for drug, alcohol, and mental health treatment; lockup provisions to incarcerate runaways; and petition processes for the Child in Need of Services (CHINS) and At-Risk Youth (ARY). CHINS petitions can be filed by a child, their parents, or the Department of Social and Human Services and are used for any youth "who is beyond the control of his or her parent," who has run away from home or out-of-home placement, and/or who is need of necessary services like food or shelter.[36] AYR petitions, which can be filed by parents, are described as focused on youth defined as: "a juvenile: (a) who is absent from home for at least seventy-two consecutive hours without consent of his or her parent; (b) who is beyond the control of his or her parent such that the child's behavior endangers the health, safety, or welfare of the child or any person; or (c) who has a substance abuse problem for which there are no pending criminal charges related to the substance abuse."[37]

In function, these systems mean that parents, youth, and social workers can enroll youth in the juvenile justice system, even when they have not been accused of delinquency. Children do not need to commit acts that would be criminal if they were adults to be justice-involved. They're not necessarily alleging that they committed a crime, and they are not asking the court system to assess status offenses. Instead, they want to enroll children in what attorneys in Washington refer to as the "civil side" of the juvenile courts—even though all of these courts are civil courts.

These provisions not only completely blur any pretense of a line between "child services" and "juvenile justice," but they also lead to greater use of the juvenile justice system in general for children in Washington. By 2011, Washington state detained 2,705 youth for status offenses, more than twice the rate of the next most detaining state.[38] Though this practice isn't uniformly practiced, the fact that it exists in any state shows how easily the systems of family policing, foster care, and juvenile justice can be interwoven. These structural similarities, when combined with the legal and public imagination, lead to certain children—children of color, Indigenous children, LGBTQ+ children, poor children, and disabled children—likely to be in the "care" of the state through foster care and/or juvenile justice, *and* they are considered inevitably criminal.

Criminalizing Children, Criminalizing Families

Children and families whose lives have been impacted by the family policing systems—whether through placement in foster care, charges in the juvenile justice system, or both—have long-reaching consequences for their lives and those of their families. Though both the juvenile justice and foster care systems were established as systems that should be used on a temporary basis to address structural issues, some children are growing up entirely within these systems. Some families have multiple generations of children raised this way, resulting in intergenerational removal from their families and communities.[39] Intergenerational child removal also increases the likelihood of a person becoming incarcerated as an adult, living in poverty, and having their own children involved in these systems.[40]

As noted earlier, foster children are more likely to become involved in the juvenile justice system. This increased risk of juvenile justice involvement and detention for foster children is also one that is directly tied to race and economic status, as can be seen by entry into the foster care and family policing systems. The best indicator of whether a child will be placed in foster care is their family of origin's income level—poorer families are most likely to have their children removed by the family policing system and placed in foster care.[41] This pattern is despite the fact that recent studies show that "unmet material needs are rarely a concern documented as a basis for [family policing] investigation."[42] What this means in practice is that the families who are most likely to be disrupted by these systems are poor and often families of color and Indigenous families, even if the system itself cannot and will not admit this through their own documentation.

Despite these known concerns with long-term involvement in the juvenile justice and foster care systems, the language around foster care, in particular, tends to focus on the need for foster homes and foster parents, not providing resources to support families of origin. In 2023, Nevada's foster care system and its challenges came into the national spotlight when news agencies reported that foster children were being housed in hotel rooms in casinos while state workers tried to find them foster home placements in rural regions of Nevada.[43] In an interview with NPR, Kevin Quint from the Nevada Division of Child and Family Services outlined a number of the challenges his division has experienced in recruiting foster parents after the COVID-19 pandemic, including COVID-19's impact, economic challenges due to inflation, recruitment of foster families slowing due to lockdowns in 2020, and the children's own needs. He reported that "the children we're getting in foster care now are coming in with higher needs, such as mental health issues and behavioral issues. And that can also be a strain on foster homes as well."[44] Here, we see not only the focus on recruiting foster parents but also framing these children as being "higher needs" children than previous generations. In the interview, he does not address whether any of those mental health needs and behavioral issues might have been caused, at least in part, *by the family policing and child removal systems themselves*. This allows the foster care and family policing systems to retain the illusion of benevolent systems.

However, even in the course of this interview that seems to largely function as a recruiting tool for foster parents, Quint highlights the importance of children staying close to their families of origin. When discussing the need for foster homes in rural areas as a high priority for his agency, Quint discusses the challenges for children who are removed from their homes. He says:

> if you have a child who's in Elko, which is northeastern Nevada, and they get placed in Pahrump, which is almost to Las Vegas, that's a whole different desert. It's a whole different, you know, landscape. And even culturally, it can be different as well. So we want to have enough homes in every community so that children can stay close to their own home. They can stay close to their school, stay close to their family. And because reunification with their birth parents is our top priority, if that's appropriate, if that's possible, then we want them to be closer to their

parents. And when they're hundreds of miles away from their parents, [that] makes it difficult to reunify because visits are hard to arrange, and it's hard to just put all those logistics together.[45]

One of the strange cognitive dissonances of working to engage critically with foster care systems is the experience of being slightly grateful for the smallest of graces, like acknowledging that moving children away from their families is bad or that family reunification is and should be the goal of any system that supports parents. However, those acknowledgments don't change the fact that in 2021, Nevada spent just under $40 million on foster care and just over $5.5 million on "prevention" services.[46] Money says as much or more than rhetoric, and it's clear that Nevada's investment is in the family policing system and not in preventing removal in the first place—that's why they need to recruit more foster families.

Conclusion

One of the core tenants of Reproductive Justice is that families of color and Indigenous families must be able to safely raise their children in their own communities. We learn a lot about which families are valued and which parents are allowed to raise their children safely when looking at the foundations of the family policing systems, as well as the places that we funnel children into from these systems—namely, foster care, and juvenile justice. Despite knowing that abuse and neglect are not limited to poor families, families of color, or Indigenous families, those are the families that are targeted by the family policing system. Those are the families whose children are more likely to be placed in foster homes or juvenile justice facilities, including Ma'khia Bryant and so many other children whose lives were made worse or ended due to these systems.

There are other worlds possible, ones that recognize all of the tenants of Reproductive Justice, ones informed by Transnational Feminisms and human rights. These worlds and systems would address financial and material realities that could support families raising children. They would also address the ongoing impacts of colonization, systematic anti-Black racism, *all* X-to-prison pipelines from schools to foster care, ableism, homophobia, and transphobia, as well as other hegemonic systems that keep the same people in power.

Children deserve more than to be the recipients of centuries of systematic violence. They also deserve more than family policing systems built on white supremacy and control. In the next chapter, we explore reimaginations of care, community, and family as alternatives to family policing, children's control, and the removal of children from family environments.

Notes

1. Nicholas Bogel-Burroughs, Ellen Barry, and Will Wright. "Ma'Khia Bryant's Journey Through Foster Care Ended with an Officer's Bullet," *The New York Times*, May 8, 2021, https://www.nytimes.com/2021/05/08/us/columbus-makhia-bryant-foster-care.html.
2. Nicquel Terry Ellis, "The foster care system is failing Black children and the death of Ma'khia Bryant is one example, experts and attorney say," *CNN Wire*, May 6, 2021, https://link-gale-com.ezproxy.gvsu.edu/apps/doc/A661706030/OVIC?u=lom_gvalleysu&sid=bookmark-OVIC&xid=e9835f35.
3. Franklin County Children's Services, "Policy 1C: Guiding principles," October 22, 2008, https://img1.wsimg.com/blobby/go/c70a9208-cb4b-415e-86b3-e16dbcb6e8c3/downloads/1C%20Guiding%20Principles.pdf?ver=1671228137478.
4. Ellis, n.p.
5. Wendyliz Martinez, "TikTok for us by us: Black girlhood, joy, and self-care," *TikTok Cultures in the United States*, edited by Trevor Boffone, Taylor & Francis Group: 39–46, 45.
6. U.S. Department of Health and Human Services Children's Bureau, *Child welfare outcomes 2007–2012: Report to Congress*, June 12, 2012, http://www.acf.hhs.gov/programs/cb/resource/cwo-07-10.
7. Hui Huang, Joseph P. Ryan, and Denise Herz, "The journey of dually-involved youth: The description and prediction of rereporting and recidivism," *Children and Youth Services Review* 34, no. 1 (2012): 254–260.
8. Craig Anne Heflinger, Celeste G. Simpkins, and Terri Combs-Orme, "Using the CBCL to determine the clinical status of children in state custody," *Children and Youth Services Review* 22, no. 1 (2000): 55–73, p. 63.
9. Stephen Wizner, "Punishing the Innocent: Juvenile Court Jurisdiction Over 'Status Offenders,'" *Journal of the American Academy of Child Psychiatry* 19, no. 2 (1980): 328–333.
10. Dorothy Roberts, "Abolish Family Policing, Too," *Dissent* 68, no. (2021): 67–69, p. 67.
11. Andrew Billingsley and Jeanne M. Giovanni, *Children of the Storm: Black Children and American Child Welfare*, Harcourt Brace: San Diego, 1972.
12. National Association of Black Social Workers, *National Association of Black Social Workers Position Statement on Inter-Racial Adoptions*, September 1972, 1.
13. e.g.: Cherie Moraga and Gloria Anzaldúa (Eds.), *This Bridge Called My Back: Writings by Radical Women of Color*, SUNY Press: Albany, 2015 and Glen Sean Coulthard, *Red Skin, White Masks: Rejecting the Colonial Politics of Recognition*, University of Minnesota Press: Minneapolis, 2014.
14. Renee Goldsmith Kasinsky, "Child neglect and 'unifit' mothers: Child savers in the progressive era and today," *Women & Criminal Justice* 6, no. 1 (1994): 97–129, p. 98.
15. Dorothy Roberts, *Shattered Bonds: The Color of Child Welfare*, (2002) New York: Basic *Civitas* Books; Walter I. Trattner, *From Poor Law to Welfare State: A History of Social Welfare in America* (1989) Chicago: University of Chicago Press.
16. Mary Kay Becker, "Washington State's New Juvenile Code: An introduction," *Gonaga Law Review* 14 (1978): 289–312, p. 290.
17. Ibid.
18. Alison G. Ivey, "Washington's Becca Bill: The costs of empowering rarents," *Seattle University Law Review* 20 (1996): 125–156.

19 Ivey, 129.
20 Shay C. Bilchik, *Addressing the needs of youth known to both the child welfare and the juvenile justice systems: Future trends in state courts* (2010) Washington, D.C.: National Center for State Courts; Marlee Kline, "Child welfare law, 'best interests of the child' ideology, and First Nations," *Osgoode Hall Law Journal 30*, vol. 2 (1992): 375–425; Rudy Estrada and Jody Marksamer, "Lesbian, gay, bisexual, and transgender young people in state custody: Making the child welfare and juvenile justice systems safe for all youth through litigation, advocacy, and education," *Temple Law Review* 79 (2006): 415–438; M. J. Higdon, "Queer teens and legislative bullies: The cruel and invidious discrimination behind heterosexist statutory rape laws," *University of California at Davis Law Review* 42 (2008): 195–253; Sarah E. Valentine, "Traditional advocacy for nontraditional youth: Rethinking best interest for the queer child," *Michigan State Law Review* 2008, vol. 4 (2009): 1053–1113.
21 Alvin L. Schorr, "The bleak prospect for public child welfare," *Social Service Review* 74, no. 1 (2000): 124–138.
22 Office of Juvenile Justice and Delinquency Prevention, "Statistical Briefing Book," January 10, 2023, https://www.ojjdp.gov/ojstatbb/court/qa06601.asp.
23 Ferguson, 2000; Hewitt et al., 2010; Meiners, 2007; Morris, 2012.
24 Victor Rios, *Punished: Policing the Lives of Black and Latino Boys*, New York University Press: New York, 2011.
25 Chesney-Lind, 2010; Males, 2010.
26 Males (2010) pp. 28.
27 Chesney-Lind, 2010).
28 Chesney-Lind, 2010, p. 60.
29 Rios, 2011, p. 27.
30 Rios, 2011.
31 Rios 2011, p. 141.
32 Jones, 2010, p. 205.
33 Jones, 2010, pp. 205–207.
34 Rios, 2011, p. xv.
35 For more information about the founding of the Becca Bill, see "Keep Becca Bill Intact," *The Seattle Times*, March 4, 1997, http://community.seattletimes.nwsource.com/archive/?date=19970304&slug=25269; Kery Murakami, "Would 'Becca Bill' have saved Becca?—Named for runaway girl who was murdered, new law gives parents more control over kids, *The Seattle Times*, June 23, 1995, http://community.seattletimes.nwsource.com/archive/?date=19950623&slug=2127830.
36 WASH. REV. CODE § 13.32A.030(3).
37 Ibid.
38 Melissa Santos, "Washington No. 1 for jailing non-criminal kids, spurred by law named for Tacoma runaway," July 13, 2015, *The News Herald*, https://www.thenewstribune.com/news/politics-government/article27129946.html.
39 For more information on multigenerational removal of children due to family policing, see Emily Putnam-Hornstein, Julie A. Cederbaum, Bryn King, Andrea L. Eastman, and Penelope K. Trickett, "A population-level and longitudinal study of adolescent mothers and intergenerational maltreatment," *American Journal of Epidemiology 181*, no. 7 (2015): 496–503; and Marny Rivera and Rita Sullivan, "Rethinking Child Welfare to Keep Families Safe and Together," *Child Welfare* 94, no. 4 (2015): 185–204.
40 Putnam-Hornstein et al.; Kathleen Wells and Maureen O. Marcenko, "Introduction to the special issue: Mothers of children in foster care," *Children and Youth Services Review 33*, no. 3 (2011): 419–423.

41 Duncan Lindsay, "Factors affecting the foster care placement decision: An analysis of national data," *American Journal of Orthopsychiatry* 61, vol. 2 (1991): 272–281.
42 Lindsey Palmer, Sarah Font, Andrea Lane Eastman, Lillie Guo, and Emily Putnam-Hornstein, "What does child protective services investigate as neglect? A population-based study," *Child maltreatment* (July 2022). doi:10.1177/10775595221114144, 6.
43 Jazmin Orozco Rodriguez, "Foster kids in Casino Hotels? It happened in Nevada amid widespread foster home shortages," *The Nevada Independent*, July 16, 2023, https://thenevadaindependent.com/article/foster-kids-in-casino-hotels-it-happened-in-nevada-amid-widespread-foster-home-shortages.
44 Scott Simon, "There's a nationwide shortage of foster care homes," *NPR*, June 15, 2023, https://www.npr.org/2023/07/15/1187929875/theres-a-nationwide-shortage-of-foster-care-families.
45 Ibid., n.p.
46 Casey Family Programs, "State-by-state Data," August 2021, https://www.casey.org/state-data/.

CREATIVE RESISTANCE FOR AND BY SYSTEMS-INVOLVED YOUNG PEOPLE

Interlude with Lizbett Benge

Lizbett values boldness, creativity, connection, joy, and transparency. She has an academic background in women of color feminisms, liberatory arts practices, and community and social change. Dr. Benge works with young, foster care systems-involved people, facilitating arts-based social-emotional learning projects and experiential political education. She loves being part of creative processes and learning *with* people. In October 2022, Lizbett initiated the first phase of her decade-long science-fiction community-based abolitionist circus dinner theatre experience. Her upcoming projects include creating queer feminist burlesque + wrestling + performance art experiences and launching Starstuff, a global arts pop-up festival.

Krista Benson: Can you share about the work you are doing now and what brought you to that work?

Lizbett Benge: I have a very fancy title, at the moment, for a job that's ending in August 2022. I am the Robert A. Oden Jr. Postdoctoral Fellow for Innovation in Humanities in the Department of Theater and Dance at Carleton College. I've taught Women, Gender, Feminist, and Sexuality Studies stuff wrapped up in a big pretty theater, performance, and movement bow. Overall, I would say I do community-based theater and teaching artistry from an intersectional feminist abolitionist lens. A teaching artist acts as a creative/maker and as an educator. I use all kinds of art and creative forms as educational tools in formal and informal learning spaces. A lot of this work has taken place with foster care systems-involved youth here in Arizona. I'm also working on putting together a burlesque troupe.

I came to this work because I spent a very long time in school, and I thought academia was the way to go, so I went. Academia felt like a safer place to me because, growing up, there were a lot of unmet needs, and a place where I found ways to meet those needs was through education. For example, there wasn't steady food to eat at home, so being part of a free and reduced breakfast [and] lunch program was cool for me. That allowed me to eat food and have consistent people around, which was also not part of my upbringing.

From the time I was young, I was very afraid of young people and babies because all I knew was, once you have a child, they get taken away. It took me a long time to get to this point of being like, "Oh yeah, I do believe in young people, and they're amazing!". Not in the sense that I preach, "Oh, bless the children, and they'll build and lead us to the future we are waiting for," because those kinds of narratives absolve adults of much of the responsibility of change, care, advocacy, preservation, and place so much burden and pressure on an entire generation to literally remake and save the world. For me, it's more about respecting the genuine learnings, insights, and creativity that young people offer to all. I had to learn that young people aren't a burden to society; they don't get taken away because there's something wrong with them, and young people as a whole aren't naïve or powerless or "stupid." Kids are not something to be scared of. I don't have to be afraid of what I don't know, and a changing world doesn't have to be a source of fear or anxiety.

There are people who can be strong, supportive role models, offer different ways of being, or model behavior that I don't think was ever really introduced to me until later in life. I'm thirty-three, so when I say later in life, I mean, like, twenty. I know. I guess this is the point where I also say that I grew up in foster care, right? That's kind of the extension of how I got to the work that I do. It felt scarier to go to school to be an artist than to learn the critical theory gender studies stuff. I figured, hey, that's the [critical theory gender studies] stuff that will help me in life and make better art. So, I went that route and got my PhD in Gender Studies.

Tanya Bakhru: What do you mean when you say "the system"? How do you use art and theater in your own practice with youth who have been impacted by foster care and other so-called systems of care?

Benge: What is the system? I will say there is a lot of imperfection and lack of precision in a lot of the language we use. I don't think that this is necessarily the best or most fitting term to say, like "systems-involved kids." Yeah. Which system? Well, as an intersectional feminist, they all work together, right? Naming one doesn't always point to the multiplicity of how these things operate or how they're co-constitutive. When I say the system, yes, I'm meaning the foster care system and maybe more broadly the umbrella of child welfare, but then there are major intersections like social welfare systems, the prison industrial complex, and the systems within capitalism. That's what I'm trying to reference when I say system or system(s)-involved. It's more about signaling certain relationships to the state and that there are lots of overlaps in how people are caught or trapped or disappeared in bureaucracy. Also, the system changes even if we just say foster care. The foster care system can and does look wildly different, even between counties. Systems [that] can be that open is a bit mind-blowing, at least for me.

How do I use art and theater in my own practice with youth who've been impacted by foster care and other so-called systems of care? I would say it's important to note that I do not pretend to practice art therapy. Art can be therapeutic, but I am not a practitioner of art therapy. My own feelings about art therapy are that it's largely still rooted in dominant systems such as racism, patriarchy, white supremacy, and settler colonialism, and there are prescriptive rehabilitative aims to it that I don't believe in either. Art therapy tends to still be wedded to the state in ways that I feel creates more harm. What I'm trying to do with art and theater, ideally, is create holistic awareness, repair harm, or maybe even recognize it. Part of that is getting in touch with one's body. Oftentimes, foster care is talked about as a traumatic experience. Like, it doesn't matter whatever happened that got you entangled in the system. Psychologists and educational experts say that even being placed in foster care is a trauma in and of itself. Cool, if we're already at some baseline assumption — this is traumatic —I gather there's going to be some manifestation of that physically in an embodied and emplaced way. I'm using art and theater to provide a way to feel ourselves, whether that be our feelings or our physical selves. Maybe there is an emotional, spiritual component, but like a really sagacious way of trying to connect. I connect to people in and through art. It's not necessarily a matter of saying, here's a picture that we've painted, and now we are going to recreate this as if it's some Paint and Sip event. It's not that; it's having a variety of materials like popsicle sticks, pipe cleaners, glitter, all kinds of paints in all kinds of colors, gems, tissue paper, beads, sand, wands, costume pieces, and construction paper, and saying to people, "Here are materials; let's create and generate something from what we have. Here are all of the tools that we have at our disposal, and let's build an environment." What is then created uses us, our voices, relationships of faith, the environment, and nature. It's as expansive as you want or need it to be. I'm working on connecting with people where there's an abrupt and kind of obvious disconnect, and that disconnect is happening through the system, foster care, or other so-called systems of care.

Benson: Can you give us some examples of projects or something that you have done with the youth? Can you give us some examples of projects you do with them?

Benge: Sometimes it's just as simple as using some tried and true theater exercises. One of them [is] a game called "Baby, I Love You, Won't You Please Smile." The "baby" can feel weird and diminutive sometimes, so we replace that word with something else. It's like, "Hey, [insert what person wants to be called], would you please, please smile?" There's someone sitting in a chair, right? Straight-faced. One person, it is their job to try and get that person to laugh. You have to do whatever you can to make that stone-cold sitter just bust their gut. Going through this exercise with young people and seeing or experiencing what they draw upon to try and get someone else to laugh is so instructive. If we're talking about points of connection, what people will tend to do, in my experience, is they will start listing out the insults. They will start talking shit about people; they will start bringing up all this past drama and gossip stuff. I'm like, "Whoa, can we do this without fatphobia?" They'll just look at me. I use it as a way to be like, "Hey, I know you're trying to make them laugh, but maybe there's another way to do it that isn't putting people down. Can we try something else? Try something new?" It's this iterative process, and finally, they get to a point where either they're super-frustrated with me, which is also real life, or they're singing old songs and quacking like ducks and rolling on the ground and trying to sniff their armpits. I find that to be a very powerful way to use art in theater. Not to punish people, right? Not to say, "Oh, stop, cut that out," right? To just ask them to try something new and point out what's at play there. It's a complex dynamic because the people I'm working with are directly impacted by racism, sexism, patriarchy, adultism, state violence, sexual violence, and poverty. So, in addition to navigating their day-to-day interpersonal worlds, they're also living out longstanding forms of discrimination and harm. What are the relationships of power there? Honestly, it's a lot of self-hating things rooted in dominant systems that come out, too. Being able to affirm or reaffirm a young person that they are who they are is oftentimes much needed. Reminding people you're going to move how you move, and that is absolutely fine. Your voice is how it is right now. You can be a boy and paint flowers and rainbows and want a Lamborghini. You come from where you come from, and there's no value statement attached to that. That's one example.

For another example: I wouldn't say I'm some formally trained dancer, but I can dance. So, music comes on. I'm going to do my thing. The young people like to move, too, because generally, the people that I work with are coming from group homes, whether they [have] to do with mental health treatment or substance use, but some regulatory kind of placements where you don't really have any solitude or privacy or space of your own. And there are tons of rules. I find music and movement to be two really rich ways to connect with people. Things like the "Cha-Cha Slide," something where I kind of know this, and it repeats itself, and we can pick it up. It's a way to build rapport without having to do gross icebreaker-y things that are tools of forced vulnerability. It's like, "Let's just move together and breathe together, and maybe we sweat a little together and have the shared experience around something that feels somewhat familiar and being able to just move in an unregulated way." I'm not trying, again, like I said, to discipline anyone in what they are doing. I will turn the music all the way up, and we will dance and then play musical chairs because there's also a fun, competitive element that they seem to gravitate towards, too. For me, it feels good to be able to play music from all around the world and different time periods and genres because, again, [there are] low-key ways of being expansive and teaching things outside of the dominant norm or even having an introduction to it. Oftentimes, I'm working with young people of color. I'm working with queer and trans people, right? And disabled folks. The group home staff will reflect that population more often than not, at least here in my experience. Again, that's because it's a very low-wage, high-energy kind of labor. It's a lot of Black women here in Arizona. I can speak about this local context, but more largely in schools or if they're judges, case managers, or case workers? No, they're going to be primarily white. If one of the kids I work with is riding in the car somewhere with a case manager, they're not likely to hear music specific to their culture or origins, for example. Again, [I draw] on points of connection and trying to work towards some version of freedom, whatever that might be.

Bakhru: I really appreciate the phrase you use, "forced vulnerability," and that you want to create points of connection without reenacting a forced vulnerability, which to me is really profound because so much of the experience of the foster care system is forced vulnerability, and also a disconnection with yourself, your family, or your community. That seems very important for a lot of different people who are involved in the system.

Benge: Yeah, thank you for reflecting that back.

Benson: You used the wordplay in a bunch of different ways: playing music, they would play with each other when they're trying to make each other laugh. Because play, to me, is also a kind of vulnerability. It's a kind of vulnerability where everybody has to be equally vulnerable, right? For example, I like hearing how you use art, theater, games, music, and dance as ways for people to be able to play. That's something that is not emphasized as being important for a lot of system-involved kids. In fact, the value of their time to play is often denied to them.

Benge: It's wild. These are still kids. I think so many people forget that in whatever way, shape, or form. I know I felt I had to be so grown up all the time. There's also a meme about this. I think someone goes, "Oh wow, you're so mature!" and in response, someone's all, "Thanks, it's my trauma!" Yes, let's play for sure.

Bakhru: Some of the things that you're saying really connect to some other Interludes we've done. For example, the idea about points of connection was discussed in one of the previous Interludes. We talked about trying to reconnect to one's humanity and trying to have other people see your own humanity. Really inherent in the foster care system is a dehumanization, not just of children, but of all different actors in the system. To laugh, to dance, to play are really human experiences, and to be able to reconnect with that embodied experience is profound. It is very deep because there are so many different layers of what you're doing that's trying to facilitate a rediscovery of one's own humanity at all different kinds of levels.

Benge: We go back to the first question, what's the work you do? Some of the work that I have done, and continue to do, but maybe not in such a forward way right now, is arts-based sexual violence awareness and prevention work. It's the best language I have for it right now. One of the projects that I did was a Skillshare addressing the everyday ways that we combat sexual violence. My response to ways we combat sexual violence was anything you do to rehumanize oneself and others, and that's vast and broad because sexual violence is an intersectional feminist issue.

Sexual violence is the destruction or distortion of a person's sense of self, most broadly—the sense of a person being a person. Sex, understood as a biological and binary category, is, in fact, expansive and mutable. Because sex is so closely linked with genitals, gender, and social roles, it really does encompass an entire human experience. Many mainstream or dominant narratives about sexual violence are often defining sexual violence, or sexual assault, or sexual abuse as unwanted or unwarranted actions of a sexual nature—as in some form of desire, gratification, and pleasure exchange—connected to one's biological sex, performed through gender and social roles, and expressed in fleshy, aesthetic, and artistic forms. While [defining] sexual violence as rape, harassment, coercion, or any form of non-consensual sexual act is not wrong or misguided, it doesn't allow for the fullness and broad scope of analysis, connection, or coalition-building that we can have otherwise. Think how various acts, policies, and ideas destroy a sense of a person being a person. Policies banning people from playing sports in gender-aligned ways—How about we get rid of these binaristic systems of categorization?—are acts of sexual violence because they deny the dignity of trans/queer peoples' lives and are harmful to a person's sense of self, as they re-entrench medically and socially inaccurate outmoded ideas of bodies, gender, and power. To me, it really is about those points of connection among ideas and others.

Benson: Also, our conversation just now speaks to how foreign these concepts are in relation to how the system is set up, right? Part of the reason we're all struggling with the language is that we're talking about things that the system is built to deny—human dignity, individuality, and connection, those are things that the system denies people. Again, not just children in the system, but all kinds of people that are connected to it.

In other conversations that we've had, you suggested an additional prong of Reproductive Justice that's focused on children's agency. Can you tell us more about how you are thinking about this idea?

Benge: Yes, and I'm happy to talk about this because, like anything, it's imperfect, and there's plenty to work through. The way I'm understanding Reproductive Justice at this point is one's ability to reproduce or not, right? To have the say in power over the kinds of conditions that one would bring this life about and sustain it. It is about maintaining bodily autonomy or, for the sake of being simple here, to have children or not. To be able to address the conditions in which one does so, and then everything to come before, after, and throughout the lifecycle of a person. Okay, where do those children actually fit in any of that? To say, like, "Hey, shouldn't I, as a child, have a stake in this too?"

I'm not a reproducer at this point and may never be in my life. In the U.S. American context, in the context of the workings of settler colonialism and patriarchal, hierarchical order, kinship structures that shape the ideas of what a household is and what bringing someone into one's family/

kin arrangement should have to be—What if these were actually mutually constituted and deeply consensual processes in as many ways and as much as possible? That's not how people tend to think, even if we're talking about foster care and adoption. I had a professor ask me, "I'm meeting a sixteen-year-old girl who's coming into the house, and I wanted to ask you—I was thinking of having some paints in the bedroom and some art supplies, and is there anything else you would suggest?" I thought it was the weirdest question because I was like, "I don't know who this person is. I don't know what to put in their room. Like, you know better than [I do]." Her question was structured around bringing this person into an already established way of being. They will assimilate, they will mold, they will do. Even though we put on the guise of "Hey, this is a shared space" or "family" for you, too, even in the framing of those questions and setting up the physical space of things didn't reflect any kind of meaningful agency or choice or consent from whoever that young person was. That might seem like a minute example, but this is how tons of people operate, whether or not we're working within the system; that is generally how the nuclear family operates. It's like my little fourth prong, something about communication and boundaries and structure and being able to cocreate or to be in a thing together and figuring it out. What are the ways we coerce people in certain ways of being based on our own projections and ideas of what/what/when/how we are? How do we create conditions of safety and love and freedom so people can have consensual co-created space and selves, [and] be in deep relationship with one another, [with]communities, pods, families, et cetera so that [we] can share the responsibilities widely and have what one needs already provided. Because it's not one size fits all. It can't be; it never will be. Well, that's my thing, right? How does that work when you have a nine-month old who can't communicate linguistically? I don't know how to address that per se, but it's a consideration.

Bakhru: I think what you are talking about is similar to the idea of legibility. Who becomes human, and who is less than fully human? What families are legible, and what families are not legible? There's a lot of connection to what you're talking about now and how children become legible in the foster care system specifically. Which children are more legible than others?

Benge: For the 2016 presidential election, I worked on a theater piece called "The Race," and it asked the question, "What do you want to see in a leader?" Part of the show was having different activities available for all the ways people might be feeling during [the] election and performance day. During the creative process, Xanthia Walker, who is the artistic director of Rising Youth Theater here in Phoenix, was like, "There are so many people who can't vote; so many different kinds of people, and how do we pretend to be a democracy when young people have no formalized democratic say about any of these large-scale decisions? What's up with this arbitrary eighteen age requirement stuff?" It was that prompting that was like, "Oh yeah, young people, especially systems-involved ones, are systematically denied access [to]so many things that are potentially life-giving or life-taking.

Bakhru: What relationship do you see between Reproductive Justice frameworks and the U.S. systems that you've outlined when you talk about systems-involved kids? How do you see these different things working together?

Benge: To be honest, Reproductive Justice, from my understanding, is built from an intersectional human rights framework. I took a class with Loretta J. Ross,[2] and this is what she communicated. I was like, "Okay, I don't know how much stock I have personally in a human rights framework being an underpinning thing on which we build, or if the ideas of rights as defined and doled out by policies and courts align with my ideas about justice." Again, the socio-juridical stuff reinforces a lot of dominant structures. Anytime you pass a law or a policy, there will always be people left out. There are so many intersections and so many experiences that get overlooked. For example, I work with a collaborator who is part of the Illinois Caucus for Adolescent Health. She didn't know I grew up in foster care. When she found out, she shared with me how a lot of the young people that she worked with at the caucus who had been in foster care had essentially been coerced into getting Depo-Provera contraceptive shots. That's concerning. This is part of the spectrum of sexual violence and reproductive subjugation that entails forced hysterectomies, sterilization of peoples without their knowledge and consent, plus disappeared children, and all of this disproportionately and intergenerationally affects Indigenous, Black, and immigrant women of color. And, of course, what of girls and those with the ability to carry a fetus, especially the ones ensnared in state care?

I experienced a similar thing when I was older. When you get a contraceptive shot, it's not something you can just, like, get out of your body. You can react in so many different ways. I bled for six months straight, and I was just like, "What the hell is going on?" If someone does respond in that way, group homes aren't necessarily set up to care for someone who might bleed perpetually for six months. There's more obvious things, like talking about the severance of parental rights, in the ways that kinship structures are obliterated by the system. There's so much around gender, sexuality, and religion, and these are all Reproductive Justice issues as well. In foster care, I don't know if I have had young people explicitly talk to me about religion. They will talk about church people who come to group homes bearing gifts and to do volunteer things. Again, how much choice and agency do they have about being exposed to whatever ideologies might be lurking under there? I don't know. What does it mean for me as an artist to be in that space? As an abolitionist, too?

I've met quite a few young moms, [and] the things that they had to experience during pregnancy writ large, shame and ridicule, and having to comport oneself in certain ways around different staff members, worrying about getting written up. Again, what are the consequences for their child once they have it? Generally, they have to move to a different kind of facility —a lot of things that one is forced to do without a system of support that might be stable in other conditions. There are still a lot of young people who adopt me or adults who start coming around. There are those questions like, "Can I come to your house?" Or they will say, "Take me home with you." I think that speaks to a desire around trying to figure out how do you want to be parented. What kind of arrangement do you want? I know this is not coming from a direct place of like, "Oh, but I think you'd be the best mom." It's probably more like, "I don't want to be in the situation I'm in. You seem safe enough," but again, even to be able to validate and recognize that might be something they're trying to communicate, it's really fucking important, and we should listen to young people. I believe they have what they need. But structurally, interpersonally, things around them are not set up for them to receive.

Benson: That connects back to what Tanya [Bakhru] was saying about some of the things that you were recognizing is especially true for children in the system, and also, it's true in a less intense or dangerous way for almost all children. We don't listen to kids as a culture. It's just much more dangerous for kids in the system, or it's dangerous in really specific ways. Children have so little control over the conditions under which they're living. One of the things when you were talking about the church ladies coming to the group home is they're the same church ladies that went to the homeless shelter that I worked at for kids who are homeless between the ages of thirteen and eighteen. Almost all of those kids were system-involved, broadly, but also former foster kids or in the care of the state because they lived in a homeless shelter.

Those are the same church ladies who volunteer in juvenile justice centers, where nearly all of the volunteer programming is provided by religiously affiliated groups. These kids, because they're multiply involved, often they're being exposed to those things in multiple places.

Benge: It's insidious. It feels important to say, if we're still using this language of humanizing and humanity, that language doesn't acknowledge our relationships to physical environments, built environments, and all that. I'll speak from my own experience that though I aged out technically at eighteen, foster care was moments in my life, and those moments have passed, but that wasn't the case at all, though. Being a former foster youth was a really strong driving narrative for me for quite some time. I'm finally at the point where I can probably release this now because I am moving on in different parts of my life.

I'm still reflecting on why this was such a part of my life for so long — what was my narrative about it and what I actually understood the impacts to be. Being in academia and having something to exploit, in a way, something that differentiated me, felt almost necessary to do. I mean, where else would I go to try and understand life and myself? School was such a big part of what I was doing in the world, trying to figure myself out, and [I found] that I needed far more support than what I got. I started to really release this narrative after COVID-19 isolation and making the decision to leave academia. I'm freer to do other work and to relearn everything all over again! As we're acknowledging these experiences, this is something that people probably know too, but it bears repeating. This could be something that impacts someone for the rest of their lives in some really fundamental ways. Foster care and adoption really benefit from a Reproductive Justice lens in the same sense we're talking about bodily autonomy and having a choice and consent throughout all parts of one's life cycle. I never thought I would make it this far. A big part of me couldn't conceptualize a certain age, and I didn't think I'd be here now. I know that's the case for some people, honestly. A lot of those driving conditions come from being in foster care, but I want to be able to conceptualize those things, think about life in a broad, holistic manner, and have hope. That's what I hope people will do as they approach Reproductive Justice, adoption, and foster care.

5
REIMAGINING CARE AND COMMUNITY

The Right to Parent

Introduction

The right to parent one's children in a safe and healthy environment is a central tenet of the Reproductive Justice framework. This principle is based on the idea that parenting is a human right, as outlined in the Universal Declaration of Human Rights (UDHR).[1] This chapter begins by exploring the idea of the right to parent being rooted in human rights discourse and demonstrates the ways in which the right to parent directly relates to the health and safety of one's communities. The right to parent in a safe and healthy environment demands that "the state not unduly interfere with women's reproductive decision making, but it also insists that the state has an obligation to help create the conditions for women to exercise their decisions without coercion and with social supports."[2] In other words, the state has a responsibility to do no harm to women and pregnant people, and at the same time, take action to support the conditions necessary for them to have reproductive freedom.

In tracing the formation of the right to parent as a human right, this chapter also addresses what it might take to fully actualize that right. The second half of this chapter highlights three movements working to stop family separation and reimagine notions of family, community, and care: these include upEND, an organization working on the abolition of the foster care system; Families Belong Together, an organization that works to permanently end family separation and detention and seeks accountability for the harm that has been done; and Movement for Family Power, an organization focused on divestment from the foster system and reinvestment in community. Through the examination of these movements, this chapter ties together the following key ideas from this book as a whole: the colonial legacy of forced family separation, the importance of the Reproductive Justice and Transnational Feminist frameworks to comprehensively understand the significance and impact of involuntary family separation, and what it means to center the right to parent as we move forward in building a new future where all children and families are truly valued.

The Right to Parent Is a Human Right

One aspect of the Reproductive Justice framework that makes it so potentially transformative is its explicit engagement with a human rights framework. The notion of human rights is rooted in the idea that there is an inherent dignity in human existence and that all people have inalienable rights. These rights serve as a foundation for freedom, justice, and peace in the world.[3] The United Nations' UDHR, along with many subsequent conventions and treaties, outlines and proclaims that societies have a responsibility to protect the freedom and dignity of human beings. Using a human rights framework is a frequent method of organization for reproductive freedom outside the United States, particularly in the Global South, but historically, it is not a prominent mechanism for reproductive rights movements within the United States. Human rights discourse has been used by many feminist movements transnationally to invoke an internationally recognized set of tenets with which to hold governments to account.

A human rights framework gives us an opportunity to examine the complicity of state and non-state actors in violations of human rights. Indeed, when discussing foster care and adoption systems in Chapter 2, we saw how the state, in conjunction with private corporations, actually benefits from the forced separation of families and the removal of children. This benefit can be monetary, as demonstrated by the success of private companies that set up detention centers for separated asylum-seeking families during the Trump Administration. However, this benefit can also be in the form of ideological gains, as seen in the propping up of racist ideology to serve a nationalist agenda about which types of family configuration are the most valid or legitimate. In Chapter 1, we also looked at the critical role that the forced separation of families played in maintaining the institution of slavery and colonization of land and natural resources, which provided tremendous wealth to both individuals and the state while ensuring white dominance in the formation of the United States itself. In contrast, human rights provide a moral baseline of accountability for what treatment one is entitled to simply by being human.

Furthermore, having and raising children, family formations, and relationships are complex. They are shaped by a variety of social factors. As Ross and Solinger state, "[N]ations, political parties, religious and ethnic groups, and other entities [all] claim a stake in reproduction."[4] The social meaning that is invested in the birthing and raising of children helps shape ideas about who should or shouldn't have children, which children are valuable to society and which are not, as well as which families are legitimate and which are not. The childbearing body exists and is imbued with social meaning. We saw examples of this in the overrepresentation of children of color, particularly Black and Native children, in the foster care system. Chapter 2 outlined the ideology, rooted in colonization and propped up by a white supremacist capitalist patriarchy, that underpins the forced separation of families over and over again throughout the formation and existence of the United States. It is apparent from these examples that the strength of a parent's right to raise their children has repeatedly been qualified by skin color and economic status.

Ross and Solinger highlight the ways that feminists in the 1970s utilized the concept of sexual citizenship, drawing on the UDHR, to assert that women's rights are human rights that include "their right to have control over and decide freely and responsibly on matters related to their sexuality, including sexual and reproductive health, free of coercion, discrimination, and violence."[5] This means that regardless of class status, race, ethnicity, sexual identity, religion, disability, caste, behavior, or any other factor, women and childbearing people must have the right to sexual and reproductive autonomy and self-determination. This includes the right to parent one's children.

But what does having a right to parent mean in real and material terms? To have a right often does not translate into the enacting or embodiment of that right. To answer this question, we can turn to the work of Sonia Correa and Rosalind Petchesky.[6] The authors write about the necessity of understanding rights in terms of power and resources, namely the power to make informed decisions about one's reproductive destiny and the resources to carry out those decisions safely and effectively. They further argue that "enabling conditions," or the provisions necessary to have the power and resources to enact one's rights, must be factored into our conceptualization and implementation of human rights.[7] In the context of the right to parent, we must ask, what does a person need to parent safely and effectively? What are the material and infrastructural supports that are required? The answer includes, but is not limited to, economic security, including a living wage, stable housing, freedom from violence, health and education services, and even political representation. As Correa and Petchesky state, "Rights not only involve personal liberties (domains where governments should leave people alone), but also social entitlements (domains where affirmative public action is required to ensure that rights are attainable by everyone)."[7] In line with this thinking, the Reproductive Justice framework demands that governments both refrain from inflicting harm and simultaneously take measures to ensure and promote the right to parent. This means that it is not enough to stop forcibly separating families. Reproductive Justice demands that governments invest resources in the supports that are necessary and effective to actively keep families together.

True control over one's reproductive destiny—including if, when, and how one parents—is essential for the well-being of the individual, family, and the community. Bodily integrity is essential to reproductive freedom. In the context of a human rights framework, bodily integrity means that bodily self-determination is a necessary basis for one's full participation in society. Furthermore, bodily integrity translates into the right to "enjoy the full potential of one's body."[8] It is a concept that sees the body as part of an integrated whole self. This sense of self is crucial not only for the individual—as we have seen throughout this book, the control of families and one's ability to not only have children but also raise those children is directly related to the outcomes of entire communities and groups of people.

The concept of the right to parent as a human right arises from discussions, interactions, and connections the founders of the Reproductive Justice movement made during their experience at the 1994 International Conference on Population and Development (ICPD). These conferences and their interaction with Reproductive Justice activists are foundational to understanding the core tenets of Reproductive Justice: the right to have a child, the right to not have a child, and the right to parent the children one already has. Historically, international discourse around reproductive matters centered on population control, putting the blame for global problems from economic insecurity to environmental crises at the feet of women in the developing world and their childbearing capacity. It was generally accepted that the solution to such problems lay in controlling their fertility. The 1994 ICPD began the shift to placing notions of empowerment at the center of reproductive health policy. This paradigm shift took place over decades and still continues to take shape. Still, it meant women's fertility and people's childbearing capacity should be seen as more than a means to an end in terms of policy formulation and implementation.

Challenging the centering of abortion to reproductive rights and fighting to end population control, such as coercive sterilization, were central to the experiences of women of color in the United States. Throughout the history of feminist organizing in the United States, instances of white women focusing on the issues most pressing for them without thinking across differences resulted in the exclusion of voices and social issues from the movement. White radical feminist groups took their experiences to represent the experiences of women as a whole, and therefore, they failed to recognize that women of color and poor women had different experiences and different problems that needed to be addressed. Throughout the second wave of feminism, women of color argued that race and class informed one's reproductive experience. Seeing themselves as embodying a unique "Third World Within" experience, U.S. women of color connected with many of the experiences of efforts of women from the Global South.[9] "Despite being in the 'first world,' their social status produced experiences and health outcomes like those of people living in 'undeveloped' nations in the 'Third World.'"[10] Contributions of women of color to discussions on reproductive politics strove to create a more inclusive movement and include issues such as sterilization abuse, pre- and post-natal health care, child care, and economic sustainability, in addition to abortion rights.[11] The understanding that "they could not separate their bodies from the context in which they were living"[12] and change needed to include broader community issues that went beyond topics traditionally categorized as reproductive activism. Out of this understanding, Reproductive Justice argues that the right to parent is directly related to the health and safety of one's communities, as the individual right relies on the latter for realization.

Case Studies

Activists and scholars are reaching a consensus that "continuing to reform the child welfare system will never make it safe for children or supportive of families. The system and its foundational logic must be completely eradicated and replaced by a radically different approach to child safety and well-being."[13] As we have shown throughout this book, foster care and adoption systems are working exactly as they were designed to do. Through the surveillance and domination of communities of color, poor people, and immigrants, forced family separation is used as a tool to control and exploit particular groups of people and maintain a hierarchy that benefits a white supremacist capitalist patriarchy. As Dorothy Roberts so thoroughly demonstrates in her meticulous research, the underpinning logic of the child welfare system is that "children's hardships are caused by parental pathologies, and child safety is achieved by policing families."[14] It is for these reasons, Roberts contends, that the multitude of reforms that have been instituted over decades of the system's existence has yet to actually solve or even reduce the instances of harm to children.[15]

The family policing system deliberately refuses to look at the issues facing vulnerable and marginalized families in a holistic and intersectional manner, something that a Reproductive Justice framework provides. Roberts cites research that shows one of the primary mechanisms to protect against the harming of children is to reduce child poverty.[16] Highlighting a 2019 study, she shows that expanding programs that give direct support to families through food, housing, and medical care subsidies—including a direct child allowance—would produce a dramatic decrease in child poverty and therefore harm to children.[17] However, programs of this kind are not only few and far between, and when enacted, they are met with incredible resistance. For example, during his first months in office, President Biden oversaw an expansion of the Child Tax Credit as part of the American Rescue Plan, providing up to $3600 to parents, including households that were previously ineligible because they reported no income.[18] The tax credit, which resulted in direct monthly payments to families, lifted approximately four million children out of poverty. Research showed that "the evidence is clear: while in place, the expanded Child Tax Credit reached the vast majority of families with low, moderate, and middle incomes; shored up family finances amidst the continuing COVID-19 and economic crisis; helped reduce child poverty to the lowest level on record; decreased food insufficiency; increased families' ability to meet their basic needs; and had no discernable negative effects on parental employment."[19] The research also showed that the long-term benefits of the policy make up for its direct cost by improving child health and education while reducing involvement with the child welfare and criminal justice systems.[20] Compare the cost of a program like the Child Tax Credit with billions of dollars spent on a child welfare system that prioritizes maintaining children outside of the home. While Biden's Child Tax Credit was by no means perfect and more was needed to make sure it was truly accessible, it was a step in the right direction toward acknowledging the interrelatedness of social issues such as access to housing, a living wage, or physical and mental health services that impact children's safety and well-being, and supporting families.

Because the so called child welfare system fails to meet its proclaimed goals and because it ultimately causes more harm than it alleviates, many are calling for the abolition of the system altogether.[21] Abolition of the child welfare system requires a reimagining of what protecting children and families actually means and looks like. This requires acknowledging that keeping children with their families and in their communities in a safe and supportive way is a basic need and right. Abolition aims to shrink the system overall while simultaneously channeling resources toward family resilience and community safety. One direct way to accomplish this is through divesting resources in the size and scope of the child welfare system and reinvesting resources in direct support to families and communities. As we have seen in this chapter, in order for the right to parent to be meaningful, one must have the power and resources to exercise it. In other words, *enabling conditions* must be in place to realize one's rights. In material terms, enabling conditions must include access to mental health services, a living wage, access to education, health care, safe housing, and child care, to name a few. The conditions must also provide protection from punitive interventions that cause more harm and trauma, as seen in family separation and its destabilizing effect on communities.[22]

A key aspect of abolishing the child welfare system is locating and generating social services from within the families and communities that are impacted. As Kelly states, "[T]hose engaged in abolition must have faith in the wisdom of the communities themselves to know and build what they need."[23] This requires a move away from reliance on an "expert" who has some kind of special knowledge that will cure perceived pathologies that run through families and therefore cause the need for state intervention. Kelly describes this shift concretely, stating:

> First, space needs to be ceded and funds need to be provided to support the generative energies of the communities that have been beset by the harms of the child welfare system. Second, to the extent that existing social service professionals continue to operate in these spaces, they need to follow the lead of the communities in which they operate, distance themselves from the punitive and coercive culture of child welfare and reorient their practices towards support and prevention.[24]

To accomplish this, the child welfare system must be decoupled from social service provision. For example, symptoms of poverty are often interpreted as neglect. This has led to over-reporting to the authorities of poor families and families of color. Requirements for mandated reporting exacerbate over-reporting due to fear on the part of professionals that they will experience negative repercussions if they do not report suspected neglect. Consequently, there is a chilling effect for families to seek out the assistance they need. For example, if parents are afraid to ask for help from teachers, health care workers, or social workers because they fear being reported for neglect, they will not do so. Social services must be provided in a way that ensures family cohesion rather than separation. This could mean relying on community-based groups to provide services, mutual aid networks, or direct payments from the federal government, like the child tax credit.[25] In other words, we must think of what kind of knowledge is needed to keep children safe and to keep families together in the greater context of their larger community. Community strategies and restorative practices that are already in place and successful need to be identified and supported.

As Loretta Ross explained, identity politics, intersectionality, and Reproductive Justice "require thinking between and beyond colonized spaces to discover new knowledges from the pain of our bodies and from the multigenerational dislocations we experienced as people of the African Diaspora."[26] She calls on the values and practices of Ubuntu as a vision of future possibilities. Translated as the concept, "I am because We are," Ubuntu recognizes the inherent value of life itself, the interdependent nature of human existence, and a simultaneous recognition of the importance of the individual and the social relationships that make up society.[27] She states,

> In terms of reproductive justice, Ubuntu offers another way of envisioning collective mothering and fathering, for example, because children are never orphans depending on a single individual or nuclear family to raise them. Instead, children are the links to our ancestors, and responsibility for their health, education, safety, and well-being rests with the community.[28]

Thinking expansively, beyond the nuclear family that is ordained through legal discourse and new social norms can allow unrecognized kin, relationships, and family to become recognizable.

In her book *Queering Family Trees: Race, Reproductive Justice and Lesbian Motherhood*, Sandra Patton-Imani argues that stratified reproduction, "the arrangements by which some reproductive futures are valued while others are despised," produces and maintains inequality in the ways different family relationship are deemed legitimate and legible.[29] She makes the point that adoption and foster care are "grounded in erasures, and the most glaring absence in this mainstream narrative is the acknowledgment of power regulating the reproductive options available to different populations of women."[30] The author suggests that by *queering* our notions of family, we can challenge, critique, and resist normative power structures that mark if and how a family is seen and if they are legible. In this way, queering the family involves making transparent the complex ways that power shapes families, as well as recognizing the symbiotic, interdependent relationship between members of a community. Embedded in Patton-Imani's idea is a challenge to the erasure and delegitimization of the multitude of relationships and connections that children and the adults in their lives have, which create notions of family. Queering the family also requires us to honor and recognize the subtle and complex relationships people have with each other, their families, and the nation by pulling back the curtain on the mechanisms of white supremacist capitalist patriarchy.[31]

The question remains: How can we as a society ensure that children are safe and looked after and that their families are supported? The analytical frame with which the issues are approached matters drastically. What is needed for children to be safe *and* for families kept together? How can women and childbearing people maintain autonomy over their reproductive destinies, including their right to have and raise children? What would this look like?

upEND[32]

UpEND is a collaborative movement started by Dr. Alan Dettlaff at the University of Houston College of Social Work. UpEND focuses on the abolition of the child welfare system. Its work is focused on divestment of and dismantling the mechanisms of family surveillance and policing and the creation of systems that support children and families. "The upEND movement seeks to identify and describe the ways in which existing child welfare policies, practices, and research support and maintain racial inequities, and to replace those with new, anti-racist responses that keep children safe and protected in their homes."[33] This movement draws a direct connection to the Reproductive Justice framework in their organizing, noting that they

> build on the work of reproductive justice, which centers bodily autonomy and asserts that parents should live in a society where they have power to make decisions about how and when they will parent and the ability to raise their families in conditions that are free of oppression. In other words, we seek to build a world where the care, support, and well-being of children, families, and communities is fully realized.[34]

UpEND draws a direct line from contemporary family surveillance, policing, and separation to the enslavement of Black people, emphasizing the white financial investment that existed in the reproductive capacity of Black women and the children they bore. They recognize that "Reproductive Justice seeks to create a world where Black children are safe, where Black self-determination is possible, and where material conditions are radically transformed in ways that support Black life" and that the family policing system actively works against such self-determination.[35] As Detlaff states, "[E]liminating racial disproportionality and disparities, and the harm they cause, will only be achieved when the forcible and involuntary separation of children from their parents is no longer viewed as an acceptable form of intervention."[36]

UpEND also works coalitionally and intersectionally by linking together a number of critical issues that must be addressed if children and families are truly going to receive the care they need. These include enacting intentionally anti-racist policies and practices around issues such as adequate, safe, and affordable housing; a guaranteed minimum income; and affordable and accessible health care.[37] They propose the following as a means to achieve their goals: 1) create and expand critical safety net programs; 2) expand the use of informal kinship care and increase concrete supports needed to care for children without child welfare intervention; 3) end the use of congregate care placements for children and youth; 4) strengthen and extend the application of active efforts standards to all cases; and 5) eliminate policies that use arbitrary timelines to terminate parental rights. They find the solutions to the harms created by the current family policing system by utilizing community-based support for families and the care of children, designed by and for the families and communities that are themselves affected. They believe the family and community should be the first line of safety and protection, not state surveillance or intervention.[38] UpEND's goal is to end institutionalization rather than to end care.

Families Belong Together[39]

Families Belong Together is a coalitional campaign that grew out of the National Domestic Workers Alliance. Organizations working together under the umbrella of Families Belong Together include the Women's Refugee Commission, MomsRising, FWD.us, the Haitian Bridge Alliance, the Texas Civil Rights Project, La Unión del Pueblo Entero, Al Otro Lado, the ACLU, MoveOn, Amnesty International, RAICES, Cameroonian American Council, Doctors for Camp Closure, and Justice for Migrant Women. The campaign was formed in 2018 in response to the Trump Administration's family separation policy, which was discussed in Chapter 1. Families Belong Together organized a nationwide protest in the summer of 2018. Over 600 marches occurred in cities across the United States, and some marches happened outside the United States, including London and Berlin, in solidarity.[40] News coverage framed the marches as targeting immigration policy, which is true, but it can also be seen as a Reproductive Justice issue linking together the disastrous impacts of global capitalism and the emergence of the corporate state, government responsibility for the social welfare of citizens and noncitizens alike, and the deeply rooted racism and sexism that props up neo-colonial efforts.

For example, in March 2019, Families Belong Together contributed to a successful pressure campaign aimed at JP Morgan and Wells Fargo, aimed at ending the financing of private prison companies Geo Group and Core Civic.[41] Both JP Morgan Chase and Wells Fargo received large contracts from the federal government to house and detain forcibly separated families during the Trump Administration's campaign against immigrant and asylum-seeking people. As was discussed in Chapter 2, the U.S. government invested billions of dollars in child detention—from housing, beds, food, and foster care to medical and psychological services, transportation, and guards. The corporations GEO Group and CoreCivic ran the majority of Immigration Customs Enforcement (ICE) detention facilities. They both donated heavily to the Trump campaign and earned over a billion dollars from ICE contracts. Through this process, corporations and the state worked together to militarize family separation and detention, generating tremendous profit in the process. Families Belong Together works to end family separation and detention, seeks accountability for the harm done, and reunites those who have been impacted by forced separation and detention.

Movement For Family Power[42]

The Movement For Family Power is an organization with the aim of defunding and divesting from the foster care system and investing in resources that are proven to support families. Founded by two lawyers, Lisa Sangoi and Erin Miles Cloud, The Movement For Family Power takes an intersectional approach to understanding foster care as a system of oppression. They draw on working collaboratively with "reproductive justice, racial justice, criminal justice, economic justice, disability justice, health care justice, drug policy reform, harm reduction, LGBTQI and immigration justice."[43] In alignment with the values of other organizations like upEND, The Movement For Family Power advocates for the centering of voices and experiences of those individuals, families, and communities that are affected by family separation and policing. They aim to challenge hegemonic notions of expertise based on title or educational degrees by acknowledging that those who are affected by family separation are experts on those issues—a key aspect of the movement for abolition, as was discussed earlier in this chapter.

One of their campaigns focuses on challenging the criminalization of pregnant people who test positive for drugs, arguing that the resulting family separation creates a "womb to foster care pipeline."[44] Along with the Bronx Defenders legal aid firm, JMacForFamilies, and the New York Drug Policy Alliance, the Movement for Family Power is campaigning for New York State Senate Bill S4821A, which would require "meaningful consent" from those giving birth before they are tested for drugs.[45] The goal is to stop the practice of hospitals making child maltreatment reports to the state hotline when a pregnant or birthing person receives positive toxicology tests, often conducted without their knowledge or consent. Those reports result in CPS investigations that can lead to newborns being taken from their mothers and parents at a critical bonding stage, and causes extensive emotional harm thereafter."[46] The campaign for Senate Bill S4821A is part of a movement recognizing that what is needed is the provision of resources to help families rather than punish or criminalize.

The criminalization of pregnant people is deeply rooted in the racial and class disparities that contextualize a spectrum of reproductive health issues and which the Reproductive Justice framework argues is absolutely necessary to understand if we are to engage in truly liberatory, transformational, and rights-based practices that honor the full humanity of all people.

Conclusion

Change is possible. It requires a reimagining of our current circumstances and compassionate action that centers the inherent dignity in life. Organizations and movements, like those mentioned in this chapter, are rethinking the role of the state and reconceptualizing who has the expertise to create the solutions needed. The rights-based, intersectional, and holistic nature of the Reproductive Justice framework is vital here. Along with analytical tools provided by Transnational Feminist frameworks—which make visible the raced, classed, and gendered ways that globalization and capitalist patriarchies (re)structure colonial and neo-colonial relations of domination and subordination—a society where children are safe and looked after and families are supported is possible.

Notes

1 UN General Assembly, *Universal Declaration of Human Rights*, 217 (III) A (Paris: UN General Assembly, December 10, 1948), https://www.un.org/en/about-us/universal-declaration-of-human-rights.
2 Loretta Ross and Rickie Solinger, *Reproductive Justice: An Introduction* (Oakland: University of California Press, 2017), 169.
3 UN General Assembly, *Universal Declaration of Human Rights*, preamble.
4 Ross and Solinger, *Reproductive Justice: An Introduction*, 168.
5 Ross and Solinger, *Reproductive Justice: An Introduction*, 179, quoting UN World Conference on Women, *Beijing Declaration and Platform for Action* (Beijing: September 4–15, 1995), https://www.un.org/en/conferences/women/beijing1995.
6 Sonia Corrêa and Rosalind Petchesky, "Reproductive and sexual rights: A feminist perspective," in *Population Policies Reconsidered*, ed. Gita Sen, Adrienne Germain and Lincoln C. Chen (Cambridge: Harvard University Press, 1994), 107–126.
7 Corrêa and Petchesky, "Reproductive and sexual rights," 107.
8 Corrêa and Petchesky, "Reproductive and sexual rights," 113.
9 Zakiya Luna, *Reproductive Rights as Human Rights* (New York: New York University Press, September 2020), 70.
10 Luna, *Reproductive Rights as Human Rights*, 70.
11 Jennifer Nelson, *Women of Color and the Reproductive Rights Movement* (New York: New York University Press, October 2003).
12 Luna, *Reproductive Rights as Human Rights*, 15.

13 Dorothy Roberts, *Torn Apart: How the Child Welfare System Destroys Black Families– and How Abolition Can Build a Safer World* (New York: Basic Books, 2022), 281.
14 Roberts, *Torn Apart*, 283.
15 Roberts, *Torn Apart*.
16 Roberts, *Torn Apart*.
17 Roberts, *Torn Apart*, 289.
18 Adam Cancryn, "Let's make a deal: White house ready to bargain over expanded child tax credit," Politico, White House, December 12, 2022, https://www.politico.com/news/2022/12/12/white-house-expanded-child-tax-credit-00073392.
19 Megan A. Curran, "Research roundup of the expanded child tax credit: One year on," *Poverty and Social Policy Report* 6, no. 9, Center on Poverty and Social Policy, Columbia University (November 15, 2022): https://www.povertycenter.columbia.edu/publication/2022/child-tax-credit/research-roundup-one-year-on.
20 Curran, "Expanded child tax credit."
21 Alan Detlaff, Kristen Weber, Maya Pendleton, Bill Bettencourt, and Leonard Burton, "What it means to abolish child welfare as we know it," *The Imprint*, October 14, 2020, https://imprintnews.org/race/what-means-abolish-child-welfare/48257#0.
22 Detlaff et al., "Abolish child welfare as we know it."
23 Lisa Kelly, "Abolition or reform: Confronting the symbiotic relationship between 'child welfare' and the Carceral state," *Stanford Journal of Civil Rights & Civil Liberties* 17, no. 2 (2021): 312.
24 Lisa Kelly, "Abolition or reform:" 316.
25 Dorothy Roberts, "I have studied child protective services for decades. It needs to be abolished," *Mother Jones*, April 5, 2022, https://www.motherjones.com/crime-justice/2022/04/abolish-child-protective-services-torn-apart-dorothy-roberts-book-excerpt/.
26 Loretta Ross, Lynn Roberts, Erika Derkas, Whitney Peoples, and Pamela Bridgewater Toure, eds., *Radical Reproductive Justice: Foundations, Theory, Practice, Critique* (New York: Feminist Press at the City University of New York, 2017), 199.
27 Ross, et al., *Radical Reproductive Justice*, 201.
28 Ross, et al., *Radical Reproductive Justice*, 201.
29 Sandra Patton-Imani, *Queering Family Trees: Race, Reproductive Justice and Lesbian Motherhood* (New York: New York University Press, June 2020), 51, quoting ed. Faye D. Ginsburg and Rayna Rapp, *Conceiving the New World Order: The Global Politics of Reproduction* (Berkeley: University of California Press, 1995), 3.
30 Patton-Imani, *Queering Family Trees*, 11.
31 Patton-Imani, *Queering Family Trees*.
32 See UpEND.org, https://upendmovement.org/about/.
33 "About," upEND.org, accessed March 1, 2023, https://upendmovement.org/about.
34 "About," upEND.org, accessed March 1, 2023, https://upendmovement.org/about.
35 "Reproductive Justice demands the end of family policing," upEnd.org, accessed March 1, 2023, https://upendmovement.org/2022/03/03/reproductive-justice-demands-the-end-of-family-policing/.
36 Alan Detlaff, Kristen Weber, Maya Pendleton, Reiko Boyd, Bill Bettencourt, "It is not a broken system, it is a system that needs to be broken: The upEND Movement to abolish the Child Welfare System," *Journal of Public Child Welfare* 14, no. 5 (2020): 509.

37 "New movement seeks to 'upEND Child Welfare System," University of Houston Graduate College of Social Work and Center for the Study of Social Policy, News and Events, accessed March 1, 2023, https://uh.edu/socialwork/_docs/Emessages/upendmovement_pressrelease.html.
38 Detlaff et al., "It is not a broken system," 511.
39 See Families Belong Together, https://familiesbelongtogether.org/about/.
40 Phil McCausland, Patricia Guadalupe and Kalhan Rosenblatt, "Thousands across U.S. join 'keep families together' March to protest family separation," NBC News, nbcnews.com, June 30, 2018, https://www.nbcnews.com/news/us-news/thousands-across-u-s-join-keep-families-together-march-protest-n888006.
41 Robert Armstrong, "JPMorgan chase axes lending to private prison operators," Financial Times, FT.com, March 5, 2019, https://www.ft.com/content/d897c034-3f7a-11e9-9bee-efab61506f44.
42 See Movement For Family Power, https://www.movementforfamilypower.org.
43 See Movement For Family Power, https://www.movementforfamilypower.org.
44 Madison Hunt, "New York campaign aims to stop 'womb-to-foster care pipeline,'" *The Imprint*, April 13, 2022, https://imprintnews.org/family/new-york-campaign-aims-to-stop-womb-to-foster-care-pipeline/64206.
45 Movement For Family Power, "'Whatever they do, I'm her comfort, I'm her protector:' How the foster system has become ground zero for the U.S. drug war," Movement For Family Power, June 2020, https://static1.squarespace.com/static/5be5ed0fd274cb7c8a5d0cba/t/5eead939ca509d4e36a89277/1592449422870/MFP+Drug+War+Foster+System+Report.pdf.
46 Movement For Family Power, "'Whatever they do.'"

VISIONS OF THE FUTURE THROUGH INDIGENOUS HUMAN RIGHTS

Interlude with Julian Aguon

Julian Aguon is a human rights lawyer and the founder of Blue Ocean Law, a progressive firm working across Oceania at the intersection of Indigenous rights and environmental justice. He is also the author of the acclaimed new book, *No Country for Eight-Spot Butterflies,* and was a Finalist for the 2022 Pulitzer Prize in Commentary.

Krista Benson: What brought you to the work that you do now? Not so much in terms of your educational journey, necessarily, but what is it that you find resonates with you about the work that you're doing now? Why did you seek out to do this kind of work?

Julian Aguon: Back in college, I had a few ideas of what I might want to do with my life. I imagined a career as a writer. I took a few of the English courses on offer, and I realized quickly that so much of what was being taught was just craft. It didn't really appeal to me because I realized rather early on that I cared less about the craft of writing and I cared more about having something worthwhile to say. After all, what does one write anyway? At the time, I was also studying Sociology and Women's Studies, which were subjects that swelled with substance—with things worth saying. I realized then and there that, while I wouldn't abandon my dream of one day being a writer, I would focus on gaining the kind of understanding that would make a difference, sharpen my critique, help me connect where we're going as a society, [and] with where we've been. That's how I viewed these other subjects: as capable of helping me ask the questions that could do the work of repairing the world. In truth, both my love of writing and thirst for feminist subjects arose out of a desire to both recognize and fight injustice, to both build and equitably distribute power. You might say that my most enduring impulse has been about this, about understanding power, about working for justice. Long story short, that's why I switched my major from English to Sociology. My truest questions were always sociological in nature. I would eventually come home to my island of Guam, freshly sobered by that critical education, and realize I walked right into a war zone. In 2005, the United States made a bilateral agreement with the government of Japan to relocate thousands of U.S. Marines from Okinawa to Guam. Okinawa being, essentially, a colony of Japan and the U.S., [which was] being forced to shoulder an inordinate amount of U.S. Military personnel and U.S. Military bases, and was experiencing a wide range of adverse impacts—from environmental contamination to extreme noise pollution to extreme acts of violence against women. Yet our own local leadership on Guam, a colonial government in its own right, was so utterly weak, so thoroughly collaborative with the U.S. federal government. It's like local leaders barely blinked an eye, accepting these Marines without question, without any semblance of concern or accountability. Back then, what was clearly happening were the harms of centuries of colonization being freshly exacerbated by the harms of militarization. And I couldn't breathe. So, I went to law school, not because I love the law—after all, the law suffers from severe limitations—but because it can be a useful tool in the toolkit. When used masterfully and tied to the broader pursuit of justice, the law can be a powerful thing. That's why many of us go to law school in the first place, to deploy the law in service of vulnerable communities and to stop those in power (e.g., the U.S. military) from running roughshod over the people. For the past decade or so, I've been trying to hold those in power to account, to hold the line, to worry the edges of our legal and political imaginations. Whether it's defending our

	local government's self-governing authority from further encroachment[1] or suing federal agencies like the United States Fish and Wildlife Service,[2] the cases I've worked on have been about that work that started back in college, that feminist work of pulling up things by the root and planting new things.
Benson:	You are a human rights lawyer, among many other things. You're also a writer and a poet. What are your thoughts on how we could use human rights concepts or structures to transform how we think about adoption and foster care systems, especially as they impact Indigenous people?
Aguon:	Wow, that's a great question. I can think of like a million people who are more qualified to answer it all because there's so many people working in this area. Off the top of my head, there's Addie Rolnick, a law professor at UNLV,[3] who is an amazing attorney who works in the areas of Indigenous rights, civil rights, and juvenile justice. Human rights are invaluable because they are a concrete mechanism by which [we] hold governments accountable for violating the rights of their citizens. Of course, this is a more complicated part of it. It can depend on what country you're in. In the United States, for example, there are very unique and curious sets of historical circumstances, how human rights law and human rights litigation has unfolded, and I'll explain it briefly so you have some context. Primarily, the New York-based Center for Constitutional Rights[4] is a bold and brilliant organization. The attorneys there basically dusted off a 200-year-old law, the Alien Tort Statute,[5] also known as the Alien Tort Claims Act, which allows claimants to bring alleged violations of human rights into the federal district courts to litigate violations of The Law of Nations.[6] The interesting issue becomes: Who is the perpetrator? The statute allows certain human rights cases to go forward in federal court, but they're invariably about human rights violations in other countries. I'm thinking now of the *Doe v. Unocal* case, which, like many of these cases, is about human rights abuses brought on by way of extractive industries, by way of oil and gas pipelines, cases where we see certain countries—never our country, just other countries—colluding with corporations.[7] What I'm trying to say is, the U.S. was, for a long time, fine

with letting these human rights cases go through, so long as the invisible finger remained firmly pointed at other countries, not the United States.

That is the first thing that you have to understand is that the mainstay of human rights litigation in this country is that it's outward looking. When it comes to looking at ourselves, we have all of these legal fictions; so many areas of American law are teeming with escape valves. Take the issue of holding the United States to its international obligations, for instance. The U.S. has signed certain human rights treaties like the International Covenant on Civil and Political Rights,[8] right? It's the only treaty it actually ratified. Yet, despite that fact, the treaty goes unenforced. Why? Because federal courts have devised this theory that certain treaties are "non-self-executing," meaning they are unenforceable in the absence of separate domestic implementing legislation. This is in spite of the textual command in the Constitution itself that treaties be considered among the "supreme" law of the land. Talk about a workaround to ensure that a treaty has no domestic legal force. Look at what's come to the fore in recent years in terms of forced removals of Indigenous children in the U.S., but also in Canada. Look at all these missing and murdered Indigenous women and children. It's clear to me that so many of these schemes, especially the forced removal of Native children, or even the forced sterilization of women, [that] these would easily meet the international definition of genocide, but the U.S. would fight that characterization tooth and nail. What I'm saying is games are afoot—in the law, as everywhere else. None of this changes the fact that, from a big-picture perspective, international law—human rights law and otherwise—fulfills an important function in that it is a normative system. It sets out a charter against which countries can be judged. I apologize if this has become too abstract an answer, but it shows you a little about how I think about these things structurally.

Another thing I want to point out is how certain legal fictions abound, particularly when it comes to how the United States has chosen to deal with various groups of Indigenous peoples it has colonized or otherwise profoundly dispossessed. Two very clear examples of how federal courts have abused their power when it comes to devising doctrine come from federal Indian law[9] (the law governing how the federal government deals with Indian Tribes) and territorial law[10] (the law governing how the federal government deals with the inhabitants of the overseas colonial possessions it acquired in the aftermath of the Spanish-American War). In both bodies of law, a disingenuous legal fiction was fashioned and deployed against these vulnerable peoples: in the case of the former, it was the legal fiction of the "domestic dependent nation"; in the latter, it was the doctrine of "territorial incorporation." In both instances, the doctrine at issue was simply made up to meet the political exigencies of the particular historical moment. And we're all still paying the price for these jurisprudential game-playing. American Indians and the peoples of the U.S. colonies are still buckling beneath the pressure of these infamous decisions hundreds of years later. Right now, tribes are still under attack in so many ways; their self-governing authority [is] under relentless attack. Most recently, we see an example of this in the *Brackeen v. Haaland* case, which involves the Indian Child Welfare Act.[11] In my own home island, Guam, we see the interlocking and compounding crises of colonization, militarization, and extensive environmental contamination. No wonder more and more people, scholars and otherwise, refer to such game-playing as lawfare. We see multiple examples here, whether it's the *Davis* case, involving the denial of the right to self-determination of the native inhabitants of Guam, or the case of *Guam v. United States*,[12] which involves liability under the Comprehensive Environmental Response, Compensation, and Liability Act (CERCLA) for a hazardous waste facility created by the U.S. Military. It is all too much to bear, yet it is the natural byproduct of this country's inability to ever deal squarely with the roots—as opposed to the branches—of its most intractable problems.

Benson: You said other people could answer that better than you, and you just gave us a whole-ass lesson in human rights, environmental degradation, genocide, and impact on indigenous communities!

Tanya Bakhru: One of the things about Reproductive Justice is a framework that I really appreciate is that it's interlocking. It's intersectional in its analysis. Things like environmental justice, reproductive rights, rights in terms of the law, sovereignty, and anti-capitalist movements, all of these things are related. The example that you gave us is a really good example of how all of those things are working together and why we need an analytic tool that's more comprehensive. This is a nuanced and complicated thing that is happening. How do we make sense of it?

Aguon: Yes, but it helps sometimes to think out loud or to lean on other thinkers, other artists, and writers capable of really big thinking. Off the top of my head, one writer who has been so helpful in honing this type of thinking is Aurora Levins Morales. Her updated and revised version of *Medicine Stories*[13] is truly something special. The introduction alone is a case study of masterful framing, and in terms of movement building, it is spellbinding in its diagnosis of where we've come and where we're going. It's really helped me think more deeply about the interlocking nature of these things.

Bakhru: What do you think restorative justice would look like for Indigenous communities around histories of family separation and other impacts of colonization?

Aguon: I really have to think about it. Perhaps the second part of the question is more answerable than the first: decolonization. I'm a proponent of decolonization. And I mean just that. Decolonization is not a metaphor, as so many Indigenous advocates have said in recent years. One book in particular that makes this point so well is *The Red Deal: Indigenous Action to Save Our Earth*.[14] I recommend it to everyone. It should be required reading. So should Roxane Dunbar-Ortiz's *An Indigenous Peoples' History of the United States*.[15] The Red Nation, which really ignited around the campaign against the Dakota Access Pipeline (the #NoDAPL movement), is doing incredible work. These activists are, like Levins-Morales, so clear in their diagnoses of the problem but also in their prescriptions. They don't hedge their bets like so many other scholars do. They call their enemy by name. They have no problem naming the perpetrator. Also, they're not busy playing that "both sides" game. And when they post things on social media like #landback or #decolonizationisnotametaphor, they mean just that. They want justice, and they want it on their own terms. In Guam, what this would look like is the

	return of huge swathes of land that was wrongfully taken from my people in the wake of World War II. It would be an internationally supervised self-determination referendum to once and for all terminate the U.S. colonization of Guam.
Benson:	The way you think has always been really illustrative for me, Julian. The clarity that you bring to the things happening in Guam, I think, is really important for us folks on the mainland to understand, and obviously, it's important for people on Guam to understand too. One of the other really substantial violences of colonization is the erasure of the colonization itself.
Aguon:	Right. As a military base and nothing else, no native population even. Just look at the language used by politicians, media, and the like. As a writer, you hone in on language. For instance, Guam is often referred to as an "unsinkable aircraft carrier," a piece of real property that can be manipulated and moved around like a chess piece. To be clear, that piece is a pawn. It is no exaggeration to say my island and my people are pawns in the war games and shenanigans of others, chief among them, the United States. That is the direct outcome, straight up, of many SCOTUS decisions.
Benson:	Yes, both legally and in the popular imagination. Often when people think of the United States, they don't even think of Hawai'i and Alaska, let alone places like Guam, American Samoa, or Puerto Rico. We talked about American colonization as if it was an event in the past. Which one? There are literally still colonies.
Aguon:	You know what's also mind-blowing? So many otherwise good and reasonable people's inability to pay attention to truly terrifying and concrete adverse impacts happening on the ground in so many places like Guam. Instead, so many reserve the lion's share of their political energy, not participating in movement building or building power, but instead sitting around criticizing books or movies. I legit saw some scholars devoting more intellectual and political energy ripping into the Disney movie, *Moana*, than doing any real work in the world.
Benson:	What relationship do you see between Reproductive Justice frameworks and how adoption and foster care systems work, as you've seen them or as you understand them?

Aguon: The framework of reproductive justice is useful not only in what Tanya said about it being interlocking but it's fertile soil for conceptual expansion. The reason why I like it is that we need soil like that. We need soil like that because we need to start planting new fucking things. With Reproductive Justice, there's potential to bring in all of these other questions that are big—questions about power, geopolitical questions. The best example I can think of off the top of my head is the Republic of the Marshall Islands,[16] and the way in which what happened there gives rise to claims for a whole wide array of reparations, including a call for Reproductive Justice. My God, I don't even know a single community on Earth with a clearer call for reproductive justice. As scholars like Holly Barker[17] and others have extensively noted, Marshallese women had to devise an entirely new language to describe the babies they were giving birth to. For instance, so-called jellyfish babies, or babies born with no bones and translucent skin, babies who died within days, if not hours. One woman described it, and I tweeted a thread about this very subject back in March of last year.[18] There were so many different types of birth defects and abnormalities, not to mention so many miscarriages. One woman talked about the fear she felt while she held her newborn baby, whose membrane or skull wasn't fully developed, that her baby's brain would fall into her lap. Stories like this abound, and they're evidence and also an indictment of the violence visited upon these people by the United States. For some historical context, between 1946 and 1958, the United States detonated some sixty-seven nuclear weapons on the Marshall Islands, subjecting the Marshallese people to widespread and arguably irreversible environmental contamination, among other things. I'm a longtime ally of the Marshallese people, who have suffered varied and severe harm at the hands of the United States during and after the Cold War. Reproductive Justice is just one feature, albeit a very important one, of the broader justice that has to date eluded the Marshallese people.

Benson: When you talk about reproductive justice as fertile soil in which to plant new things, we talked about decolonization, and that's a tangible fucking action. Are there other things that you would like to see grow in that soil that have to do with human rights?

Aguon: I would like the United States to take a multidimensional approach to reparations for the Marshallese people, and by that, of course, I mean more than just monetary compensation. To be clear, the Marshallese deserve a hell of a lot of that, too. The United States could simply start by paying out all the outstanding awards issued by the Nuclear Claims Tribunal.[19] I would also make a massive investment in the health services offered to the people, both at home in the Marshall Islands and in the United States, as so many Marshallese are now part of the diaspora living in Guam, Hawaii, and certain states like Arkansas. I'd also like those services to include a full suite of services related to cancers, as, last I checked, there wasn't a single oncologist on the islands. Moreover, I'd like those islands and atolls that remain too contaminated to live on at present to be completely remediated—at no cost to the government of the Marshall Islands. I'd like the United States to take full and unequivocal responsibility to clean up the nuclear waste facility known as the Runit Dome[20] (and known to the locals as The Tomb). I'd like all of this now, and this is only a start.

I'm talking about massive investment. I'm talking about improving the quality of their lives. I'm talking about social, cultural, gender, economic, and environmental justice. All of it.

Bakhru: I'm reminded of the extent to which corporations and the state are intertwined, especially in terms of the United States. It's really a corporate state. A lot of these violations of human rights that occur—I'm thinking in terms of family separation, specifically, but I'm sure there are many other examples—are really driven and continue to go on because of investment by private money, and the benefit of private money from those violent actions.

Notes

1 Davis *v.* Guam, 932 F.3d 822 (9th Cir. 2019).
2 Center for Biological Diversity *v.* Debra Haaland et al., No. 1:2021cv00017 (D. Guam, 2021).
3 Addie C. Rolnick, San Manuel Band of Mission Indians Professor of Law at University of Nevada Las Vegas. See UNLV.com, William S. Boyd School of Law, accessed March 28, 2023, https://law.unlv.edu/faculty/addie-rolnick.

4 See "What We Do," Center for Constitutional Rights, ccrjustice.org, accessed March 28, 2023, https://ccrjustice.org/home/what-we-do.
5 Alien Tort Claims Act of 1948, 28 U.S.C. § 1350; ATS.
6 See Emer de Vattel, *The Law of Nations: Or, Principles of the Law of Nature Applied to the Conduct and Affairs of Nations and Sovereigns*, ed. Bela Kapossy (Indianapolis: The Liberty Fund, 2008). The author held that sovereign nation-states are equal, independent, and to hold rights as an individual would. The treatise is credited with shaping modern international law through the application of natural law to international relations.
7 See Doe *v.* Unocal, 395 F.3d 932 (9th Cir. 2002). The landmark decision held that corporations and their officers can be held liable under the Alien Tort Statute for violations of international human rights in foreign countries. It also concluded that U.S. courts can adjudicate such claims. The plaintiff's claims of human rights abuses by Unocal Corporation in Burma were eventually settled out of court, ending in a historic payment.
8 See *International Covenant on Civil and Political Rights*, 19 December 1966, 999 UNTS 171, Can TS 1966 No 29 arts 7-9 (entered into force April 24, 1964). The multilateral treaty holds that nations must respect certain civil and political rights of individuals, including freedom of assembly, speech, and religion, the right to life, due process and fair trial.
9 The complex body of United States law regulating the legal relationships between Indian Tribes within its borders, the federal government and individual state governments, comprising treaties, statues, executive orders, administrative decisions, and court cases. For the general principles of Federal Indian Law, see "General Principles of Federal Indian Law," University of Alaska Fairbanks, uaf.edu, accessed March 28, 2023, https://uaf.edu/tribal/academics/112/unit-4/generalprinciplesoffederalindianlaw.php.
10 U.S. federal territorial law contends with the degree to which federal law can be imposed on incorporated and unincorporated territories. In the former case, the Supreme Court has held that the Constitution is fully extended, and only partially in the latter.
11 See Brackeen *v.* Haaland, No. 18-11479 (5th Cir. 2021). The state of Texas placed a Navajo/Cherokee child with the Brackeen family, who then sought to terminate the parental rights of the biological parents. They were challenged by the Navajo Nation under the provisions of the Indian Child Welfare Act (ICWA) which gives presumptive jurisdiction over placement of American Indian children to tribal governments. The Brackeens, joined by other plaintiffs, now seek to declare the ICWA unconstitutional. Oral arguments were heard before the Supreme Court on November 9, 2022, and a decision is expected in spring 2023.
12 Guam *v.* United States, 141 S.Ct.1608 (2021).
13 Aurora Levins Morales, *Medicine Stories: Essays for Radicals* (Durham: Duke University Press, April, 2019).
14 The Red Nation, *The Real Deal: Indigenous Action to Save Our Earth* (Brooklyn: Common Notions, April 2021).
15 Roxanne Dunbar-Ortiz, *An Indigenous Peoples' History of the United States* (New York: Beacon Press, August 11, 2015).
16 The U.S. conducted 67 nuclear weapons tests between 1948 to 1956, resulting in negative reproductive health outcomes of Marshallese women to this day, yet they still encounter serious barriers to accessing healthcare, including being barred from Medicaid and Medicare, despite paying taxes.
17 Holly M. Barker, Teaching Professor, University of Washington, Department of Anthropology, accessed March 30, 2023, https://anthropology.washington.edu/people/holly-m-barker.

18 Julian Aguon (@julian_aguon), "Rongelapese women began experiencing frightening rates of stillbirths & miscarriages...," *Twitter*, February 28, 2022, https://twitter.com/uriohau/status/1628575147195269120.
19 The Marshall Islands Nuclear Claims Tribunal is an arbitration commission established in 1988 between the Marshall Islands and the United States to render final determination on claims relating to the American nuclear testing program.
20 The Runit Dome is a nuclear containment structure on Runit Island in the Enewetak Atoll in the Marshall Islands. It was built in 1977 as a temporary measure for containing nuclear damage from weapons testing during 1946 and 1958.

INDEX

Note: Page numbers followed by "n" refers notes.

ableism 4, 101
abortion 24, 121; adoption and 86; constitutional rights to 7–8, 122
ADHD 49
adoptable 65, 67, 68, 72–74, 81
Adopted and Fostered Adults of the African Diaspora 19
Adoption Fantasies: The Fetishization of Asian Adoptees from Girlhood to Womanhood (McKee) 78, 80
Adoption Resource Exchange Network of America (ARENA) 66, 68, 69
Africa 3
African American 4, 60
African Diaspora 19, 125
Aguon, J. 132–140; about 132–134; on framework of reproductive justice 136–137; on reproductive justice and decolonization 139–140; on reproductive justice in adoption and foster care 138–139; on restorative justice for Indigenous communities 137–138; on use of human rights concepts to transform life in adoption and foster care 134–136; on violences of colonization in Guam 138

Alabama 32
Alaska 42, 43, 138
Albright, M. 27–28
Alien Tort Statute 134, 141n7
Alliance for the Study of Adoption and Culture (ASAC) 19
Al Otro Lado 127
American Civil Liberties Union (ACLU) 30–31, 127
American Food Fight (Gibney) 16
American Rescue Plan 123
Amnesty International 127
Ann Arbor, Michigan 16, 21
anti-Black racism 63, 70, 101
Arbenz, J. 36
Arkansas 140
Asia 3, 80, 81
Asian Americans 63, 64
The Atlantic 29–30
At-Risk Youth (ARY) 98

Bakhru, S. 6, 20, 24, 45, 46, 50, 53, 54, 59, 79, 83, 84, 88, 90, 110, 111, 113, 114, 137, 140
Barker, H. 139
Becca Bill 98
Benge, L. 105–117; about work 105–106; on forced vulnerability 110; on humanizing and

humanity 116–117; on legibility 113–114; on projects done with youth 108–110; on reproductive justice frameworks and U.S. systems 114–116; on sexual violence 111–112; on systems of care and the systems 107–108, 112–113; on wordplay 110–111
benign paternalism 4
Berlin, Germany 127
Biden, J. 123
Billingsley, A. 93
bipolar disorder (BPD) 47
Black Americans 69
Black families 10, 27, 33, 93
Black women 24, 97; in America 5, 10, 110; racist characterizations 32; reproductive capacity of 126; reproductive labor 26; sexuality 32; violence of family separation towards 35
Borger, J. 36
Brackeen v. Haaland case 87, 136, 141n11
Briggs, L. 3, 31, 34
Bryant, M. 91–92, 101
Bureau of Indian Affairs (BIA) 64–65, 67–69, 72
Bush administration 29, 35

Cameroonian American Council 127
Canada 135
capitalism 1–2, 5–7, 38, 45, 50, 53, 60, 62, 64, 73, 74, 84, 107, 127; colonial 61; hyper-capitalism 28–29, 35–36; racialized 62
care and community 13–14, 118–129; case studies 122–126; Families Belong Together (coalitional campaign) 127–128; Movement For Family Power (organization) 128–129; right to parent as human right 119–122; upEND 126–127
Caucasian Americans 71
Caucasian Korean 71
Center for Constitutional Rights, New York 134
Central America 31, 36–37
Cherokee Nation 76n26
Child in Need of Services (CHINS) 98

child removal 1–2, 8, 11, 19, 24, 68, 95, 99, 100
children of color 3, 8, 12, 60–61, 69, 72–73, 85, 99, 120
Children of the Storm: Black Children and American Child Welfare (Billingsley and Giovanni) 93
child saving 4, 61, 65, 96–99
child-taking systems 3–4
Child Tax Credit 123–124
Child Welfare League of America (CWLA) 64–69, 72–73
child welfare system 3, 11, 18, 26, 33, 37, 65, 72, 93, 123; abolishing 124; defined 92; family policing and 92; officials 66; reformers 94; service agencies 67; system 92
China 61, 82, 84
choice 55, 56, 113, 115, 117; to advocate for justice 2; for desperate migrants 29; free choice 5; reproductive health in 5; strategic 23; of youth 97
Chung, N. 16, 21
Civilization Fund Act (1819) 34
classism 4, 24
Cloud, E. M. 128
colonialism 1, 4, 5, 27, 53, 62, 73; imperialism and 43, 51; neo-colonialism 84; settler 10, 87, 107, 112
colonization 2, 27, 101, 133, 136; globalization/capitalist 6, 10; of Guam by U.S. 138; of Native American land 33; slavery and 119
Community Health Association of Spokane (CHAS) 49, 59n6
Comprehensive Environmental Response, Compensation, and Liability Act (CERCLA) 136
contemporary child-saving 96–99; *see also* child saving
Convention Concerning the Powers of Authorities 38
Convention on the Prevention and Punishment of the Crime of Genocide 38
Cook County, Illinois 94
Corrêa, S. 120
COVID-19 pandemic 95, 100, 117, 123

criminalizing children 99–101
criminalizing families 99–101
Critical Adoption Studies 1–2, 17, 19, 61, 62, 87

Dakota Access Pipeline (the #NoDAPL movement) 137
Davis case 136
decolonization 137, 139
Degrees of Difference: Reflections of Women of Color on Graduate School (McKee) 78
Department of Health and Human Services 37
Dettlaff, A. 126
de Vattel, E. 141n6
Dickerson, C. 29
Disrupting Kinship: Transnational Politics of Korean Adoption in the United States (McKee) 78, 79
Dobbs v. Jackson Women's Health Organization 7–10, 86
Doctors for Camp Closure 127
Doe v. Unocal 134, 141n7
Dorow, S. 81
Dream Country (Gibney) 16, 21
Dunbar-Ortiz, R. 137

Eastern Europe 28
Ehlers-Danlos Syndrome (EDS) 51–52, 59n7
El Paso, Texas 29
El Salvador 31, 36
enabling conditions 120, 124
enslavement 10, 27; of Black people 126; family separation and 31–33
Europe 28, 85

Facism: A Warning (Albright) 27–28
Families Belong Together (organization) 13
family court 3, 94–95
family policing 26–27
family separation 1, 7, 38; enslavement and 31–33; forced 29; Indian boarding schools and 33–35; Iñupiaq 42–59; policy 27–31; violence of 35
Fanshel, D. 69
Flores Agreement (1997) 30
Flores Settlement Agreement 30

foster care 1, 12–13; history of 3–4; human right and 20; systems of care in 10–11; in United States 2, 3, 85, 92, 93; *see also* systems of care in foster care and adoption
foster parents 46–47, 55–56, 100
Franklin County Children's Services (FCCS) 91
Frontier Behavioral Health 47, 59n5
FWD.us 127

Geographies of Kinship (Liem) 79
Gibney, S. 16–24; about 16–17; on adoptee and adoption 17–18; on adoption and foster care 18–20; on embodied experience 20; reproductive justice frameworks and adoption foster care systems in the U.S. 23–24; on speculative fiction 23; on writing of books from early age 20–23
Giovanni, J. M. 93
The Girl I Am, Was, and Never Will Be (Gibney) 16, 17, 21, 22
globalization 5–6, 10, 30–31, 38, 83, 129
Global South 6, 119, 122
González, N. 30
Good Shepherd Home 43
Graves, K. 80
Guam 133, 136, 138, 140
Guam v. United States 136
Guatemala 31, 36
Gupta, S. 22

Haaland v. Brakeen 9, 62
Haiti 85, 88
Haitian Bridge Alliance 127
Hammonds, J. 91
Hawai'i 138, 140
Hedman, B. 98
Help Me to Find My People (Williams) 33
Hernandez, L. H. 36
HIV/AIDS pandemic 6
Homeland Security Act (2002) 30
homophobia 4, 101
Honduras 31, 36
Hübinette, T. 80

human right 134–136, 141n7; discourse 118, 119; foster care and 20; intersectional 114; reproductive justice 84, 85; right to parent as 119–122; of women 8, 120

Immigration Customs Enforcement (ICE) 37, 128
India 9, 18, 21
Indiana 9
Indian Adoption Project (IAP) 2, 11, 62–68
Indian boarding schools 10–11, 27, 33–35, 38, 68
Indian Child Welfare Act (ICWA) 7–10, 43, 45, 46, 53, 56, 59n3, 62, 87, 136, 141n11
Indian Country 72
Indigenous and Korean Children in White Families 72–74
Indigenous children 2–3, 9, 11–12, 42, 45–46, 50, 60–64, 69–72, 74, 93, 99, 135
Indigenous communities 48, 53, 65, 67, 71, 136–137
Indigenous people 1–2, 31, 34–35, 50, 52, 61, 93, 96, 134–135, 137
An Indigenous Peoples' History of the United States (Dunbar-Ortiz) 137
Indigenous sovereignty 11–12, 60, 69, 71
International Conference on Population and Development (ICPD) 6, 121
International Covenant on Civil and Political Rights 38, 135, 141n8
International Social Service (ISS) 63, 64, 70, 73
Iñupiaq family separation 42–59

Jacobson, H. 81
JaeRan Kim 23
Japan 133
JMacForFamilies 128
Jones, N. 97
JP Morgan Chase 127
Justice for Migrant Women 127
juvenile justice 2–4, 12–13, 91–93, 98–101, 116, 134; in United States 94–95

Kapossy, B. 141n6
Kelly, L. 124
Kiana, Alaska 43
Kim, E. J. 80, 83
Klein, N. 28
Klein, W. C. 71
Korea 64
Korean Adoption Project 11, 62–68
Korean War 2, 11, 61, 64

Latin America 3, 38
La Unión del Pueblo Entero 127
Law Applicable in Respect of the Protection of Infants 38
The Law of Nations: Or, Principles of the Law of Nature Applied to the Conduct and Affairs of Nations and Sovereigns (de Vattel and Kapossy) 134, 141n6
LGBTQ+ 95, 99
LGBTQI 128
Liem, D. B. 79
London, England 127
Louisiana 9, 32

Marshall Islands 139, 140, 142n20
Marshall Islands Nuclear Claims Tribunal 140, 142n19
Martinez, W. 92
McKee, K. D. 19, 22, 61, 78–90; on adoptive parents 89–90; on conceptualize care 90; on country fees for adoption 88–89; on economy of the reunion industry 82–83; on education 78; on facilitating foster care placement of children 88; on international adoption 79; on reproductive justice framework 84–88; on research trajectory 79–81; on transnational adoption industrial complex 81–82, 84
Medicine Stories (Morales) 137
Minneapolis, Minnesota 17
Moana (movie) 138
Mohanty, C. 6, 27
MomsRising 127
Morales, A. L. 137
Movement for Family Power (organization) 13, 128
MoveOn 127

National Council for Black Social
    Workers 93
National Domestic Workers Alliance 127
nationality 68–72
Navajo Nation 141n11
Negro 70
Negro Americans 71
Nelson, K. P. 60, 62, 80, 83
Nevada 100, 101
New Mexico 29
New York 134
New York Drug Policy Alliance 128
New York State 128
No Country for Eight-Spot Butterflies
    (Aguon) 132
*No Is Not Enough: Resisting Trump's
    Shock Politics and Winning the
    World We Need* (Klein) 28
non-Indigenous Americans 76n26
North Korea 28
Nuclear Claims Tribunal 140

Obama administration 29, 35
Oden, R. A. 105
Oglesby, E. 31
Oh, A. 80
Okinawa 133
oppression 5, 10, 126, 128
originalism 8

Palmer, C. 21
parens patriae 94–95
parent/parenting 61, 93, 118; adoptive
    60, 63, 64, 67–73, 79–81,
    84–85, 89–90, 98; biological
    47; child care and 8; forced
    separation of children 27; foster
    46, 47, 55–56, 100; good 61;
    immigrants 86; Indigenous 46,
    49; migration to United States
    30; Negro 70; right to 13;
    separation of 32, 34; white 43,
    47, 55, 71, 72, 78
Parents to Adopt Minority Youngsters
    (PAMY) 73
Pate, S. 80, 81
paternalism, benign 4
Patton-Imani, S. 125
Pedro, T. S. 57
people of color 1–2, 10, 38, 61, 93, 110
Petchesky, R. 120
the Philippines 28

Planned Parenthood v. Casey 7
Powers, E. 21
Pratt, R. H. 34
Progressive Era 12
Protecting Young Victims from
    Sexual Abuse and Safe Sport
    Authorization Act of 2017
    59n9
Puerto Rico 138

queering 125
*Queering Family Trees: Race,
    Reproductive Justice and
    Lesbian Motherhood* (Patton-
    Imani) 125
Quint, K. 100

racism 4, 17, 24, 29, 32, 36, 38, 64,
    101, 107, 109, 127; anti-Black
    63, 70; colorism and 71;
    systemic 1, 2
RAICES 127
Ramos, R. 42–59; on abolitionist
    movement 53; about 42;
    Ehlers-Danlos Syndrome
    51–52; family information
    43–44; on foster care system
    57–58; on foster parents
    55–57; ICWA 46; on paying
    of foster parents to take care
    of children 47; on radical love
    and interdependency 54–55; on
    relationship between foster care
    and intergenerational trauma
    49–50; on restorative justice for
    Native communities 50–53; on
    Revised Code of Washington
    (RCW) 45–46; on trauma 48
*The Red Deal: Indigenous Action to
    Save Our Earth* 137
Reid, J. 64
Revised Code of Washington (RCW)
    45, 59n3
Riben, M. 81
right to parent 13–14, 84; as human
    right 2, 119–122
Roberts, D. 3, 18, 92, 122
Rolnick, A. 134
Ross, L. 120, 124
Ross, L. J. 114
Runit Dome 140, 142n20
Russia 28, 61

Sabraw, D. 30
Sam and the Incredible African and American Food Fight (Gibney) 16, 21
Samoa 138
Sangoi, L. 128
See No Color (Gibney) 16, 17
Senate Bill 5439 98
Senate Bill S4821A 128
Sessions, J. 29
sexism 4, 5, 10, 24, 38, 109, 127
Seymore, M. 8
Shattered Bonds (Roberts) 18
slavery 5, 10, 31–33, 35, 119
social reformers 94
social services 28, 63–64, 67, 70, 124
Solinger, R. 120
South Korea 62, 73, 84–85
sovereignty 68–72, 137; Indigenous 9, 60, 71; tribal 72
Spokane, Washington 43
Spokane Mental Health 48
The Stork Market: America's Multibillion Dollar Unregulated Adoption Industry (Riben) 81
systemic racism 1–2; *see also* racism
systems of care in foster care and adoption 10–11, 26–39, 108; family separation and enslavement 31–33; family separation and Indian boarding schools 33–35; family separation policy 27–31; Indian boarding schools 33–35

Talisman, S. 70
TallBear, K. 71
Texas 9
Texas Civil Rights Project 127
The World Conference on Women in 1995 6
Third World Within 122
transnational adoption 11–12, 60–74; adoptable 72–74; domestic foster care 3; Indian Adoption Project 62–68; Indigenous and Korean Children in White Families 72–74; industrial complex 78–90; Korean Adoption Project 62–68; nationality 68–72; project of Korean "orphans" into United States 2; sovereignty 68–72

transnational feminisms 1–2, 6; reproductive justice and 4–7, 29
Transnational Feminist 2, 6, 7, 10–13, 27, 37–38, 119, 129
transracial adoption 17–18, 60–64, 69, 72, 74, 93
Trump, D. 28
Trump administration 27, 29, 30, 31, 35, 36, 37–38, 119, 127
Turitz, Z. 67, 72–73
Turkey 28
Twitter 88

Ubuntu 125
Ukraine 85
United Nations 6
United Nations Convention on the Rights of the Child 38
United Nations Universal Declaration of Human Rights (UDHR) 13, 38, 118–120
United States 7, 24, 29, 30, 31, 34, 37, 81; adoption in 2, 12; adoptive homes in 73–74; Asian American racialization in 64; authoritarianism 27–28; bilateral agreement with Japan 133; biological parent 71; Black women in 5, 10; children of immigrant parents 86–87; colonization 27; criminalization and punishment of youth in 96; *Dobbs v. Jackson Women's Health Organization* 7–10; experiences of women of color in 121; families and homes in 11; family court systems in 3, 94–95; family separation of migrants from Central America 37; federal territorial law 141n10; forced family separation 29; forced separation of families during enslavement 33; foster care in 2, 3, 85, 92, 93; illegal immigration 29–30; immigration of family from India 21; imperialism in 4, 11; Indigenous children 64; international adoptees 82; international obligations of 135; juvenile justice system 4, 92, 94–95; militarism in 61; neoliberal terrorism

27; non-citizenship in 73; nuclear testing program in Marshall Islands 142n19; nuclear weapons donated by 139; nuclear weapons tests 141n16; racial capitalist power structure 27; reparations for the Marshallese people 140; reproductive freedom outside 119; reproductive injustice in 35; reproductive justice in 6; sovereignty 37; transnational adoption in 60–62; transnational transracial adoption 63; white homes in 74; women of color 122
United States Center for SafeSport 59n9
United States Children's Bureau 61
United States Fish and Wildlife Service 134
United States Social Forum 24, 25n10
upEND (organization) 13
Urban Native Youth Organization 42
Urgent Care 49
USians 94
U.S. Marines 133
U.S.-Mexico 86
U.S. Military 133
U.S. Supreme Court 7, 9, 86, 141n10–11
Utica, New York 21

Walker, X. 114
Washington State 45, 46, 98, 99
Washington State Indian Welfare Act 59n1, 59n3
Wells Fargo 127
When We Become Ours: A YA Adoptee Anthology (Gibney) 16, 23
Where We Come From (Gibney) 16, 21
white children 12, 33, 85; non-white children 73
white supremacy 5, 7, 10, 27, 87, 101, 107
Williams, A. 32
Williams, H. A. 33
women of color 26, 93, 105, 115, 121–122
Women's Refugee Commission 127
Woo, S. 80, 81
World War II 60–61, 138

youth control complex 96